A.W. TOZER
ON
WORSHIP AND ENTERTAINMENT

TOZER

on

WORSHIP
AND
ENTERTAINMENT

SELECTED EXCERPTS

Compiled by
JAMES L. SNYDER

WingSpread Publishers
Camp Hill, Pennsylvania

WingSpread Publishers
3825 Hartzdale Drive · Camp Hill, PA 17011
www.wingspreadpublishers.com

A division of Zur Ltd.

Tozer on Worship and Entertainment
ISBN: 978-1-60066-103-7
LOC Control Number: 2006923566
© 1997 by Zur Ltd.

Previously published by Christian Publications, Inc.
First Christian Publications Edition 1997
First WingSpread Publishers Edition 2006

Cover design by
Design Source Creative Services, Inc.

Scripture taken from the
Holy Bible: King James Version

Contents

Part 3: Entertainment

Part 4: Essay by A.W. Tozer

Preface

Toward the end of his ministry Dr. A.W. Tozer commented that the war was lost, referring to the atrocious invasion of the world into the church. He objected to anemic Christianity. "In many churches," Tozer complained, "Christianity has been watered down until the solution is so weak that if it were poison it would not hurt anyone, and if it were medicine it would not cure anyone!"

A radical statement, but reading this book will clarify just what Tozer meant.

Here in one volume is a collection of Tozer's thoughts on the vitally important subject of worship—and its corruption by what he referred to as "the great god Entertainment." I have culled from my extensive library of some 500 tape-recordings of Tozer preaching to his Chicago congregation, camp meetings, conventions, his denomination's General Council and his last years at the Avenue Road Church in Toronto. One thing I noticed from his sermons was the consistency of his convictions on this subject. The year might be 1954 or 1962 but there was a harmony of thought. His were not mere off-the-cuff remarks.

At the end of this book is the essay "The Menace of the Religious Movie," which cost Tozer some friends. It has long been out of print and not many are anxious to bring it to light. However, following the logic of his conviction he does make sense. You may not agree, but you will recognize that he knows what he believes and why he believes it.

Sometimes a preacher can get carried away in his preaching and say things he really does not believe. This was never the case with Tozer. Throughout this book you will notice that the excerpts from his messages—and they are verbatim—are quite similar to what he allows in print.

The extensiveness of the quotations precludes any accusations of unscrupulous editing. After reading this book, you will have a clear picture of Tozer's convictions on these subjects. Again, you may not agree, but it should give you something to think about considering the decadent condition of the contemporary church.

The only hope for modern Christianity, Tozer contends, is in the individual. In this vein he speaks and writes, always on the lookout for people to join his Fellowship of the Burning Heart. If one person would come into the light by his preaching or writing that was reward enough for Dr. Tozer.

Rev. James L. Snyder
1997

Chapter 1

The Act and Object of Worship

Psalm 45

The impulse to worship is universal. If there is a race or tribe anywhere in the world that does not worship it has not been discovered. And yet the act of worship is, for the most part, so imperfect, so impure and so far astray that any teaching that might help us worship God more acceptably would indeed be a word well spoken.

The Act of Worship

There are ingredients that make up worship. One is admiration. We can admire without worshiping but we cannot worship without admiring, because worship is admiration carried to infinitude. In the same way, we can honor what we do not worship but we cannot worship the one we do not honor. So worship carries with it an ingredient of honor.

Then there is the spirit we call fascination. We can only worship that which fascinates us. The old poet said in an often-quoted passage, "In our astonished reverence, we confess Thy uncreated loveliness." There is an astonishment about reverence. If you can explain it, you cannot worship it. You may admire it, you may honor it, but there is a mysterious fascination that carries the heart beyond itself and then we are nearer to worship.

Another ingredient, which perhaps should have been mentioned first, is love. We can love without worshiping but we cannot worship without loving. Then love, when it lets itself go and no longer has any restraints, becomes adoration.

We need to refine our definitions. Such words as *honor*, *love* and *adore* don't mean what they are supposed to mean. We use divine language in such a common way that when we try to rise to the exalted and divine level we find ourselves using words that do not express anything. If I had the power, I would pass a law permitting the use of such words as *love*, *honor* and *adore* only in prayer, Bible teaching, preaching and song. We have spoiled them and made them common, yet they belong to God.

Worship seeks union with its beloved, and an active effort to close the gap between the heart and the God it adores is worship at its best.

The Object of Worship

The object of worship, of course, is God. The Nicene Creed says that we worship "one God, the

Father Almighty, Maker of heaven and earth, and of all things visible and invisible." That is who we worship. If we could set forth all God's attributes and tell all that God is we would fall on our knees, undoubtedly, in adoring worship. It says in the Bible that He "dwells in light unapproachable whom no man can see or has seen or can see and live" (1 Timothy 6:16, Exodus 33:20, author's paraphrase). It says that God is holy, eternal, omniscient, omnipotent and sovereign and that He has a thousand sovereign attributes. And all these should humble us and bring us down. I cannot accept with any sympathy the idea that we go to church to soothe ourselves and calm our spirits. We do calm our spirits and there is a soothing effect in worship, but the primary object of church attendance is not to relax—it is to offer worship, which belongs to God.

David sees this God incarnated in Psalm 45. He sees Him as God of the substance of His Father, born before the world was and made as the substance of his mother born in due time—a radiantly beautiful, romantic and winsome figure. And here are some adjectives he used to describe this man who is God and this God who became man: fair, kingly, gracious, majestic, true, meek, righteous, loving, glad and fragrant.

Certainly this is not the stern-browed Jupiter or Thor sitting in some high Olympus. Here is a fragrant, glad, loving, righteous, friendly God—yet majestic, "dwelling in the light which no man can approach unto" (1 Timothy 6:16), inspiring awe in His enemies and terror in His foes. This is the God we adore. Here is the Lord, "Worship thou him" (Psalm 45:11).

Even announcing that we are going to preach about worship must start the wings of the seraphim in heaven to waving and the organs to playing, because heaven exists to worship God. The atmosphere and the very breezes that flow out of heaven are filled with divine worship.

The health of the world is worship. When intelligent, moral creatures are in tune in worship, we have the symphony of creation. But anywhere there is not worship, there is discord and broken strings. When all the full redeemed universe is back once more worshiping God in full voice, happily and willingly, then we will see the new creation—the new heaven and the new earth.

In the meantime you and I, belonging to another creation, are called upon to worship God. And it says, "He is thy Lord; and worship thou him" (Psalm 45:11).

Worship must be all—entire. By that I mean that the total life must worship God. The whole personality has to worship God or our worship is not perfect. Faith, love, obedience, loyalty, high conduct and life all must be taken as burnt offerings and offered to God. If there is anything in me that does not worship God, then there is nothing in me that worships God perfectly.

I would not go so far as to say that God will not accept anything less than perfect worship; if I did, I would rule myself out. We would all hang "our harps on the willows" and refuse to "sing the LORD's song in a strange land" (Psalm 137:2, 4). But the ideal God sets before us is that we should worship as near to perfectly as we can. And if there are areas in my being which are not harmonious and do not worship God then there is no area in my being that worships God perfectly.

There is a great delusion among religiously inclined people these days. We imagine that a sense of sublimity is worship. I happen to be reading, or trying to read, a book called *Nature Mysticism*, written by some old fellow with a doctor of divinity degree. I find it hard going—not because it's profound, but because I don't agree with it. He should have known better than to write that book. In it he talks about the sublime but he doesn't talk about Jesus or God or the blood or the incarnation—only the sublime. We are supposed to walk out under the stars and feel a sense of sublimity like a crackpot poet, and that is supposed to be worship. I do not believe it.

A man—utterly corrupt, crawling with the maggots of iniquity—may feel a sense of sublimity when the great thunderstorm breaks on the mountain or when the sea in the storm booms on the shore or when the stars in their silver beauty shine at night. When you walk into a cathedral where bank upon bank of candles burn fitfully and where there are sections you can't enter, that throws over some people a sense of awe and sublimity. Awe and sublimity are ingredients of worship if the worship is there. But we can be awestruck and not worship God. We can sense the sublime and not be worshiping God.

There are poets whose faculties for the sublime were developed far beyond yours and mine. And yet they dared to write that there was no God. The Roman poet Lucretius, in his great work on the nature of things, launches into beautiful passages. He was a man in rapport with the universe, without any doubt. But he was flatly against belief in God or belief in any gods, although he was a Roman. A man who doesn't believe in God cannot worship God.

But some sissified mentality might say, "Now, just a minute, don't be so severe, dear brother. Maybe we worship God and don't know that we worship Him." If you take the Bible for it, we have to say such a thing is impossible. You cannot worship God when at the same time you do not believe He exists.

The sense of awe we feel in the presence of death, in the wonders of nature or in the silence of the night is natural, but it is not necessarily *spiritual*, though it can be. A man filled with the Spirit who has met God in a living encounter can worship God in the silence and in the storm. Spurgeon preached a great sermon on God in the silence and God in the storm. It's all true. The heart that knows God can find God everywhere. But the heart that doesn't know God can feel the emotions of nature worship without rising to spiritual worship at all.

I repeat that no worship is wholly pleasing to God till there is nothing in us displeasing God. If this disillusions anybody I do not apologize. Some of us need to be disillusioned so that we might get straightened out. A little boy may run around the house believing he's Hopalong Cassidy. He may do that up to the age of ten. But if he's eighteen and is still running around with a Hopalong Cassidy hat on, somebody needs to disillusion that boy. He doesn't need consolation—he needs to be disillusioned.

In the dawn of the race men worshiped the sun and the stars. They got down on their knees and prayed to the bushes and the trees and the mountain peaks. But we are not in the dawn of the race; we are at full maturity. Christianity and Judaism have been in the world now for thousands of years. Science and philosophy and education and progress have surely brought us to a point where at least we're able to know we are not Hopalong Cassidy. Even if we aren't Christians we ought to know that much. Instead of consoling men who believe they are worshiping God when they are not, we ought to disillusion them and show them they are not worshiping God acceptably.

No Magic Formula

Remember, there is no magic in faith or in names. You can name the name of Jesus a thousand times; but if you will not follow the nature of Jesus the name of Jesus will not mean anything to you. We cannot worship God and live after our own nature. It is when God's nature and our nature begin to harmonize that the power of the name of God begins to operate within us. As it was said so quaintly of Samson that "the Spirit of the LORD began to move him at times in the camp of Dan" (Judges 13:25), I believe that God's people ought to be moved at times to true worship. But we cannot pray toward the east and walk toward the west and then hope for harmony in our being. We cannot pray in love and live in hate and still think we are worshiping God.

Let us suppose we are back in the old days of the high priest, who took incense into the sanctum and went behind the veil and offered it there. And let us suppose that rubber—the worst-smelling thing I can think of when it burns—had been available in those days. Let us suppose that chips of rubber had been mixed with the incense, so that instead of the pure smoke of the spices filling the temple with sweet perfume, there had been the black, angry, rancid smell of rubber mixed with it. How could a priest worship God by mixing with the sweet-smelling ingredients some foul ingredient that would be a stench in the nostrils of priest and people?

So how can we worship God acceptably when there is within our nature something that, when it catches on fire, gives off not a *fragrance* but a *smell*? How can we hope to worship God acceptably when there is something in our nature which is undisciplined, uncorrected, unpurged, unpurified—which is evil and which will not and cannot worship God acceptably? Even granted that a man with evil ingredients in his nature might with some part of him worship God half acceptably, what kind of a way is that to live?

Believe it or not, I would like to be decent and nice. If I could, I would join Norman Vincent Peale in thinking about roses and symphony orchestras. But I can't join the good brother. So I've got to tell you that if you do not worship God seven days a week, you do not worship Him on one day a week. There is no such thing known in heaven as Sunday worship unless it is accompanied by Monday worship and Tuesday worship and so on.

Too many of us discharge our obligations to God Almighty in one day, usually by a trip to church. Sometimes nobly we make it two trips to church. But it's all on the same day when we've nothing else to do—and that is supposed to be worship. I will grant that it *can be* true worship, provided on Monday and Saturday we were also worshiping God.

You don't need to be in church—you can worship God at your desk; you can worship God on an elevated train or driving in traffic; you can worship God washing dishes or ironing clothing; you can worship God in school or on the basketball court. You can worship God in whatever activities are legitimate and right and good; you need not be in church all the time. How could you be?

Our Lord Himself went to the synagogue or

the temple, as His custom was, on the Sabbath day. Other days He was a carpenter and worked and shaved and sawed and drove nails with His supposed father. Like the Jew He was, He went one day a week and worshiped. Certain other times He went for a whole eight days at a stretch. But He went only one day out of the week to worship in the temple.

We can go to church and worship. But if we go to church and worship one day it's not true worship unless it is followed by worship six days after that till the next Sabbath comes. We must never rest until everything inside us worships God.

I get on a spiritual plateau every once in a while, where I seem to have learned all I can learn and risen as high as I can go. My capacity is filled for the time being, and I don't make any progress; I beat the air. Then God does something for me and I reach a new level. I think I have reached a new level recently and I'd like to share it with you.

I have been thinking recently about how important my thoughts are. I don't have to *do* wrong to get under blistering conviction and repent. I can lose the fellowship of God and a sense of His presence and a sense of spirituality by just *thinking* wrong. God has been saying to me, "I dwell in your thoughts. Make your thoughts a sanctuary in which I can dwell. See to it." You can't do anything with your heart—that is too deep—but you can control your thoughts.

So I've been trying to make my thoughts right.

When I think of people who dislike me or whom I dislike, I have tried to think cheerfully and charitably about them, in order that God could dwell in my thoughts.

God won't dwell in spiteful thoughts, polluted thoughts, lustful thoughts, covetous thoughts or prideful thoughts. He will only dwell in meek, pure, charitable, clean and loving thoughts. He will dwell in positive thoughts—even aggressive, fighting thoughts, if need be—but they must be pure thoughts, thoughts that are like God's. God will dwell in them as a sanctuary.

Your theology is your foundation. The superstructure is your spiritual experience built on that foundation. But the high bell towers where the carillons are—those are your thoughts. And if you keep those thoughts pure the chimes can be heard ringing out "Holy, Holy, Holy" on the morning air.

Make your thoughts a sanctuary God can inhabit, and don't let any of the rest of your life dishonor God. See to it that not a foot of ground is unholy. See to it that every hour and every place is given over to God, and you will worship Him and He will accept it.

And the most beautiful thing is that He will be accepting your worship when you don't know it's rising to Him. He'll be smelling the incense of your high intention even when you are snowed under by the cares of this life—even when the telephone jangling and appointments to be made and people to see keep you from thinking about

Him. If God knows your intention is to worship Him with every part of your being, God will be smelling the incense of your holy intention even if the world for a time claims your legitimate interest.

We can attain to this by cooperating with God. On God's side is love, grace, atonement, promises, the Holy Ghost; on our side is determination, seeking, yielding, believing. And our hearts then become sanctuaries where a continuous, unbroken fellowship of communion and worship is rising to God all the time. Even when you are embroiled in earthly activities, at the same time your whole life can be a fragrant altar of worship that pleases God.

Worship

Man's Reason for Being

The primary purpose of God in creation was to prepare moral beings spiritually and intellectually capable of worshiping Him. This has been so widely accepted by theologians and Bible expositors through the centuries that I shall make no attempt to prove it here. It is fully taught in the Scriptures and demonstrated abundantly in the lives of the saints. We may safely receive it as axiomatic and go on from there. (*Born after Midnight*, p. 123)

Priority in Worship

I am going to say something to you which will sound strange. It even sounds strange to me as I say it, because we are not used to hearing it within our Christian fellowships. We are saved to worship God. All that Christ has done for us in the past and all that He is doing now leads to this one end. . . .

There is a necessity for true worship among us. If God is who He says He is and if we are the believing people of God we claim to be, we must worship Him. I do not believe that we will ever truly delight in the adoring worship of God if we have never met Him in personal, spiritual experience through the new birth from above, wrought by the Holy Spirit of God Himself! . . .

I have come to believe that when we are worshiping—and it could be right at the drill in the factory—if the love of God is in us and the Spirit of God is breathing praise within us, all the musical instruments in heaven are suddenly playing in full support. (*Whatever Happened to Worship?*, pp. 94, 118, 123)

A Concept of Worship

I can offer no worship wholly pleasing to God if I know that I am harboring elements in my life that are displeasing to Him. I cannot truly and joyfully worship God on Sunday and not worship Him on Monday. I cannot worship God with a glad song on Sunday and then knowingly displease Him in my business dealings on Monday and Tuesday.

I repeat my view of worship—*no worship is wholly pleasing to God until there is nothing in me displeasing to God.* (*Whatever Happened to Worship?*, pp. 124-125)

Worship Never Cultivates Passivity

The beautiful part of worship is that it prepares

you and enables you to zero in on the important things that must be done for God. Listen to me! Practically every great deed done in the church of Christ all the way back to the apostle Paul was done by people blazing with the radiant worship of their God. A survey of church history will prove that it was those who were the yearning worshipers who also became the great workers. Those great saints whose hymns we so tenderly sing were active in their faith to the point that we must wonder how they ever did it. The great hospitals have grown out of the hearts of worshiping men. The mental institutions grew out of the hearts of worshiping and compassionate men and women. We should say, too, that wherever the church has come out of her lethargy, rising from her sleep and into the tides of revival and spiritual renewal, always the worshipers were back of it. (*Whatever Happened to Worship?*, pp. 18-19)

Our Worship Lacks Depth

It is certainly true that hardly anything is missing from our churches these days—except the most important thing. We are missing the genuine and sacred offering of ourselves and our worship to the God and Father of our Lord Jesus Christ. . . .

If we are truly among the worshipers we will not be spending our time with carnal or worldly religious projects. . . .

God has provided His salvation that we might be, individually and personally, vibrant children of God, loving God with all our hearts and worshiping Him in the beauty of holiness. This does not mean, and I am not saying, that we must all worship alike. The Holy Spirit does not operate by anyone's preconceived idea of formula. But this I know: when the Holy Spirit or God comes among us with His anointing, we become worshiping people. This may be hard for some to admit. But when we are truly worshiping and adoring the God of all grace and of all love and of all mercy and of all truth, we may not be quiet enough to please everyone. (*Whatever Happened to Worship?*, pp. 9, 12, 14)

First Things First

We all should be willing to work for the Lord, but it is a matter of grace on God's part. I am of the opinion that we should not be concerned about working for God until we have learned the meaning and the delight of worshiping Him. A worshiper can work with eternal quality in his work. But a worker who does not worship is only piling up wood, hay and stubble for the time when God sets the world on fire. I fear that there are many professing Christians who do not want to hear such statements about their "busy schedule," but it is the truth. God is trying to call us back to that for which He created us—to worship Him and to enjoy Him forever! It is then, out of our deep worship, that we do His work. . . .

I can safely say, on the authority of all that is revealed in the Word of God, that any man or woman on this earth who is bored and turned off by worship is not ready for heaven. . . .

I wish that we might get back to worship again. Then when people come into the church they will instantly sense that they have come among holy people, God's people. They can testify, "Of a truth God is in this place." . . .

True worship of God must be a constant and consistent attitude or state of mind within the believer. It will always be a sustained and blessed acknowledgment of love and adoration, subject in this life to degrees of perfection and intensity. . . .

Men and women continue to try to persuade themselves that there are many forms and ways that seem right in worship. But God in His revelation has told us that He is spirit and those who worship Him must worship Him in spirit and in truth. God takes the matter of worship out of the hands of men and puts it in the hands of the Holy Spirit. . . .

We must humbly worship God in spirit and in truth. Each one of us stands before the truth to be judged. Is it not now plain that the presence and the power of the Holy Spirit of God, far from being an optional luxury in our Christian lives, is a necessity. . . .

Yes, worship of the loving God is man's whole reason for existence. That is why we are born and that is why we are born again from above. That is why we were created and that is why we have been recreated. That is why there was a genesis at the beginning, and that is why there is a regenesis, called regeneration. That is also why there is a church. The Christian church exists to worship God first of all. Everything else must come second or third or fourth or fifth. . . .

Worship must always come from an inward attitude. It embodies a number of factors, including the mental, spiritual and emotional. You may not at times worship with the same degree of wonder and love that you do at other times, but the attitude and the state of mind are consistent if you are worshiping the Lord. . . .

Real worship is, among other things, a feeling about the Lord our God. It is in our hearts. And we must be willing to express it in an appropriate manner. We can express our worship to God in many ways. But if we love the Lord and are led by His Holy Spirit, our worship will always bring a delighted sense of admiring awe and a sincere humility on our part.

The proud and lofty man or woman cannot worship God any more acceptably than can the proud devil himself. There must be humility in the heart of the person who would worship God in spirit and in truth. . . .

They can change the expressions in the hymnals, but whenever men and women are lost in worship they will cry out, "Oh God, thou art my God; early will I seek thee" (Psalm 63:1). Worship becomes a completely personal love experience between God and the worshiper. It was like that with David, with Isaiah, with Paul. It is like that with all whose desire has been to possess God. . . .

What we need among us is a genuine visitation of the Spirit. We need a sudden bestowment of the spirit of worship among God's people. (*Whatever Happened to Worship?*, pp. 12, 13, 20, 24, 44, 46, 56, 83, 84, 89, 91)

A Challenge to Worship

Every great spiritual work from Paul to this hour has sprung out of spiritual experiences that made worshipers. Unless we are worshipers, we are simply religious dancing mice, moving around in a circle getting nowhere. . . .

God wants worshipers first. Jesus did not redeem us to make us workers; He redeemed us to make us worshipers. And then, out of the blazing worship of our hearts springs our work. (Sermon to Youth for Christ, National Convention of YFC, Chicago)

Worship Is the Center

Israel began her history in a burst of divine power. When God led the Children of Israel out of Egypt . . . and into the Holy land, with the fire and cloud going before and the children of Israel . . . one miracle followed another and grace upon grace, with faith and love and worship at the center like a beating heart. (Sermon, "The Deeper Life," Chicago, 1956)

The Definition of Worship

Worship is to feel in the heart and express in an appropriate manner a humbling but delightful sense of admiring awe. Worship humbles you. The proud man can't worship God any more than the proud devil can worship God. There must be humility in the heart before there can be worship. If it isn't mysterious there can be no worship. If God can be understood by me than I cannot worship God. ("The Chief End of Man," Sermon #5, Toronto, 1962)

God wants us to worship Him. The God who doesn't need anything nevertheless wants worshipers. The God who in His uncreated nature is self-sufficient yet wants us to worship Him. . . .

If man had not fallen then worship would have been the most natural thing to him in the world because God made man to worship Him. Man fell away and sin came to his life and sin is not natural. . . .

Worship is unnatural only in the sense that so few people really do it. But it is natural in that it is what God created us for. That's what He meant us to do, to worship Him and enjoy Him forever. . . .

I find that when people haven't found God and do not know the new birth and the Spirit is not on them, yet they have the ancient impulse to worship something. If they're not educated they kill a chicken and put a funny thing on their head and dance around. If they are educated they write poetry. ("The Chief End of Man," Sermon #3, Toronto, 1962)

The reason that Jesus Christ was born of the virgin Mary to suffer under Pontius Pilate to be crucified, dead and buried, the reason that He overcame the sharpness of death and rose again from the grave is that He might make worshipers out of rebels. . . .

Worship is the moral imperative of the Christian and yet it is the missing jewel in evangelical circles. . . .

God wants you to worship Him and then out of your fiery worship He wants you to work for Him. But He doesn't want you to jump up and start any amateurish toil. . . .

If worship bores you, you are not ready for heaven. . . .

Worship is the normal employment of moral beings. Every glimpse that we have of heaven shows the creatures there worshiping. . . . ("The Chief End of Man," Sermon #4, Toronto, 1962)

God is infinitely more concerned that He have worshipers then that He have workers. We have degenerated into the place where we put God on charity and make Him to be a foreman who can't find help. He stands at the wayside asking, "How many helpers will come to My rescue and come and do My work?" If we could only remember that God doesn't need anybody here—God does not need anybody in this city. ("The Chief End of Man," Sermon #4, Toronto, 1962)

When a man yielding and believing the truth of

God is filled with the Spirit of God then his warmest and smallest whisper will be worship. We can find that we can worship God by any means if we are full of the Spirit and yielded to the truth. But when we are neither yielded to the truth nor full of the Spirit then the so-called worship is not worship at all. ("The Chief End of Man," Sermon #3, Toronto, 1962)

We have everything but worship these days. A man you can't get to a prayer meeting will sit on the board and decide how much money the church spends. You can't get him to prayer meeting because he's not a worshiper. He's just a fellow who runs the church. It seems to me that it has always been a frightful incongruity that men who do not pray and who do not worship are nevertheless able to run the church and determine the direction it will take. No man has any right to debate an issue or vote on it unless he is a praying man. We tend to let the women do the praying and the men do the voting. ("The Chief End of Man," Sermon #4, Toronto, 1962)

Worship is an inward attitude, not a physical attitude but an inward attitude, and it is a state of mind and it is a sustained act. This is subject to degrees of perfection and intensity. You cannot always worship with the same degree of wonder and love that you do at other times, but it must always be there—an attitude and a state of mind and a sustained act subject to varying degrees of intensity and perfection. ("The Chief End of Man," Sermon # 5, Toronto, 1962)

Some of the great advances in civilization were made by worshiping men and women. Wherever the church came out of her lethargy and rose from her sleep and into a renaissance or revival, always some worshipers were back of it all. We are called to worship and we are failing God in this. We are not worshiping God as we should. ("The Chief End of Man," Sermon #4, Toronto, 1962)

God has created us that we might be worshipers and we have become everything else but worshipers.

One of the ingredients in worship is boundless confidence in the character of God. We can't worship these days because we do not have a high enough opinion of God. God has been reduced, modified, edited, changed and amended until He is not the God Isaiah saw high and lifted up but something else. Because He has been reduced in the minds of the people we don't have that boundless confidence in His character that we used to have. Confidence is necessary to respect. You can't respect a man in whom you have no confidence. When you extend that upward to God, if you cannot respect God, you cannot worship God. Worship rises and falls in the church altogether depending on whether the idea of God is low or high. ("The Chief End of Man," Sermon #5, Toronto, 1962)

I believe that when we worship our God the breath of song on earth starts the organs playing in heaven above. . . .

There can be only one worship. We cannot worship whom we will for there is only One to worship. ("The Chief End of Man," Sermon #6, Toronto, 1962)

If I haven't absolute confidence in God I can't worship Him. You can't sit down with a man and have fellowship with him if you have reason to fear that he's out to get you and that he's tricking you or deceiving you or cheating you. You have to respect him before you can sit down with him quietly. You have to trust him before you can have human fellowship. ("The Chief End of Man," Sermon #5, Toronto, 1962)

We come into God's house and say, "The Lord is in His holy temple, let us all kneel before Him." Very nice. I think it's nice to start a service that way once in a while. But when any of you men enter your office Monday morning at 9 o'clock, if you can't walk into that office and say, "The Lord is in my office, let all the world be silent before Him," then you are not worshiping the Lord on Sunday. If you can't worship Him on Monday you didn't worship Him on Sunday. If you don't worship Him on Saturday you are not in very good shape to worship Him on Sunday. ("The Chief End of Man," Sermon #6, Toronto, 1962)

God is spirit and worship must accord with the nature of God. We worship God according to what God is and not according to what God is not. . . .

Spirituality is one of the ingredients of worship, and without spirituality I cannot worship God acceptably. No matter how much I worship, if it is not acceptable worship then it is vain worship and better not attempted. . . .

A second ingredient in worship is sincerity as distinct from formality or duplicity. . . .

Honesty is a third ingredient of worship and must be in all prayers as distinct from mere propriety. I've got to be absolutely honest. There must be complete honesty before God. . . . ("The Chief End of Man," Sermon #8, Toronto, 1962)

A local church exists to do—corporately what each should do individually—namely, worship God. It should show forth the excellencies of Him who has called us out of darkness into His marvelous light, reflect back the glory of Him who shines down on us, even God, even Christ, even the Holy Ghost. ("The Chief End of Man," Sermon #10, Toronto, 1962)

Nobody has ever worshiped God and done nothing else. That's the beautiful thing about it: If you worship God, you will be an active person. Practically every deed done in the church of Christ back to St. Paul was done by people blazing with the radiant worship of God. The great mystics and the great hymn writers and the great worshipers were also the great workers. The great saints whose hymns we so tenderly sing were active to the point where you would wonder how they ever did it. George Whitefield, John and Charles Wesley, St. Bernard, Tersteegen and Zinzendorf and you can name them off. They were the ones who wrote our hymns of praise and the ones whose knuckles were skinned and whose hands and palms were callused with toil. ("The Chief End of Man," Sermon #4, Toronto, 1962)

Worship is to feel in your heart and express in some appropriate manner a humbling but delightful sense of admiring awe and astonished wonder and overpowering love in the presence of that most ancient Mystery, that Majesty which philosophers call the First Cause but which we call Our Father Which Art in Heaven. . . .

A great Christian of nearly 300 years ago, Nicholas Herman of Lorraine [Brother Lawrence] said that in his early Christian life he determined to cut through the tangle of religious means and "nourish his heart on high thoughts of God." I have always treasured that expression. A cultivation of God through prayer, humble soul-searching and avid feasting upon the Scriptures would go far to awaken the church. As long as God is considered to be very much like the rest of us, except a little higher and a little greater, there won't be any great amount of holy fear among church people. In my opinion, the great single need of the moment is that lighthearted superficial religionists be struck down with a vision of God high and lifted up, with His train filling the temple. The holy art of worship seems to have passed away like the Shekinah glory from the tabernacle. As a result, we are left to our own devices and forced to make up the lack of spontaneous worship by bringing in countless cheap and tawdry activities to hold the attention of the church people. (*Keys to the Deeper Life*, pp. 80, 88)

He [Brother Lawrence] spent his long life walking in the presence of his Lord, and when he came to die there was no need for any particular change in his occupation. At the last hour someone asked him what was going on in his thoughts as death approached. He replied simply: "I am doing what I shall do through all eternity—blessing God, praising God, adoring God, giving Him the love of my whole heart. It is our one business, my brethren, to worship Him and love Him without thought of anything else." (*The Price of Neglect*, p. 23)

The Altar Within

In our present-day age of grace and mercy, we acknowledge that the only altar in effect for us is in the glory world. It is there that our Lord Jesus Christ ministers as our great High Priest. But we are Christian believers intent upon glorifying God and worshiping Him. It is consistent with that objective that there should be an altar deep within our own hearts, our inner beings. (*Men Who Met God*, p. 29)

Worship Key to Revival

Many of the Lord's people do not know what you mean when you mention a spirit of worship in the church. They are poor victims of boards, churches, denominations and pastors who have made the noble decision to modify the truth and practice a little. But God responded, "If you do, I will withdraw from you the spirit of worship. I will remove your candlestick." (*Rut, Rot or Revival*, pp. 167, 170)

Knowledge, Wonder, Love

While we may worship (and thousands of Christians do) without the use of any formal creed, it is impossible to worship acceptably without some knowledge of the One we seek to worship. And that knowledge is our creed whether it is ever formalized or not. It is not enough to say that we may have a mystical or numinous experience of God without any doctrinal knowledge and that is sufficient. No, it is not sufficient. We must worship in truth as well as in spirit; and truth can be stated and when it is stated it becomes creed. . . .

[One] stage of true worship is wonder. Here the mind ceases to understand and goes over to a kind of delightful astonishment. Carlyle said that worship is "transcendent wonder," a degree of wonder without limit and beyond expression. That kind of worship is found throughout the Bible (though it is only fair to say that the lesser degrees of worship are found there also). Abraham fell on his face in holy wonderment and God spoke to him. Moses hid his face before the presence of God in the burning bush. Paul could hardly tell whether he was in or out of the body when he was allowed to see the unspeakable glories of the third heaven. When John saw Jesus walking among His churches, he fell at His feet as dead. We cite these as a few examples; the list is long in the biblical record. (*That Incredible Christian*, pp. 21, 128)

The essence of spiritual worship is to love supremely, to trust confidently, to pray without ceasing and to seek to be Christlike and holy and to do all the good we can for Christ's sake. How impossible for anyone to hinder that kind of "practice." As soon as our normal churchgoing religion is interdicted by government decree or made for the time impossible by circumstances, we can retire to the sanctuary of our own hearts and worship God acceptably till He sees fit to change the circumstances and allow us to resume the outward practice of our faith. But the fire has not gone out on the altar of our heart in the meantime; and we have learned the sweet secret of submission and trust, a lesson we could not have learned any other way. (*The Root of the Righteous*, p. 130)

It is quite impossible to worship God without loving Him. Scripture and reason agree to declare this. And God is never satisfied with anything less than all: "all thy heart . . . all thy soul . . . all thy might." This may not at first be possible, but deeper experience with God will prepare us for it, and the inward operations of the Holy Spirit will enable us after a while to offer Him such a poured-out fullness of love. (*That Incredible Christian*, p. 126)

Man is a worshiper and only in the spirit of worship does he find release for all the powers of his amazing intellect. (*God Tells the Man Who Cares*, p. 103)

It remains only to be said that worship . . . is almost (though, thank God, not quite) a forgotten art in our day. For whatever we can say of modern Bible-believing Christians, it can hardly be denied that we are not remarkable for our spirit of worship. The gospel as preached by good men in our times may save souls, but it does not create worshipers. Our meetings are characterized by cordiality, humor, affability, zeal and high animal spirits; but hardly anywhere do we find gatherings marked by the overshadowing presence of God. We manage to get along on correct doctrine, fast tunes, pleasing personalities and religious amusements. How few, how pitifully few are the enraptured souls who languish for love of Christ. The sweet "madness" that visited such men as Bernard and St. Francis and Richard Rolle and Jonathan Edwards and Samuel Rutherford is scarcely known today. The passionate adorations of Teresa and Madame Guyon are a thing of the past. Christianity has fallen into the hands of leaders who knew not Joseph. The very memory of better days is slowly passing from us and a new type of religious person is emerging. How is the gold tarnished and the silver become lead! (*That Incredible Christian*, p. 131)

One of the most liberating declarations in the New Testament is this: "The true worshipers shall worship the Father in spirit and in truth: for the Father seeketh such to worship him. God is a Spirit: and they that worship him must worship him in spirit and in truth" (John 4:23-24). Here the nature of worship is shown to be wholly spiritual. True religion is removed from diet and days, from garments and ceremonies, and placed where it belongs—in the union of the spirit of man with the Spirit of God. From man's standpoint the most tragic loss suffered in the Fall was the vacating of this inner sanctum by the Spirit of God. At the far-in hidden center of man's being is a bush fitted to be the dwelling place of the Triune God. There God planned to rest and glow with moral and spiritual fire. Man by his sin forfeited this indescribably wonderful privilege and must now dwell there alone. For so intimately private is the place that no creature can intrude; no one can enter but Christ, and He will enter only by the invitation of faith. "Behold, I stand at the door, and knock: if any man hear my voice, and open the door, I will come in to him, and will sup with him, and he with me" (Revelation 3:20). (*Man: The Dwelling Place of God*, p. 10)

Man Created for Worship

God is real. He is real in the absolute and final sense that nothing else is. All other reality is contingent upon His. The great Reality is God, the Author of that lower and dependent reality which makes up the sum of created things, including ourselves. God has objective existence independent of and apart from any notions which we may have concerning Him. The worshiping heart does not create its Object. It finds Him here when it wakes from its moral slumber in the morning of its regeneration. . . .

In our desire after God let us keep always in mind that God also has desire, and His desire is toward the sons of men, and more particularly toward those sons of men who will make the once-for-all decision to exalt Him over all. Such as these are precious to God above all treasures of earth or sea. In them God finds a theater where He can display His exceeding kindness toward us in Christ Jesus. With them God can walk unhindered; toward them He can act like the God He is. (*The Pursuit of God*, pp. 50, 98)

Longing for God

When all of the fully-redeemed universe is back once more worshiping God in full voice, happily

and willingly and out of the heart, then we will
see the new creation and the new heaven and the
new earth! Worship seeks union with its beloved,
and an active effort to close the gap between the
heart and the God it adores is worship at its best.
(*The Tozer Pulpit*, Book 1, p. 56)

Brethren, when we finally have our meeting
with God, it has to be alone in the depths of our
being. We will be alone even if we are surrounded
by a crowd. God has to cut every maverick out of
the herd and brand him all alone. It isn't something that God can do for us en masse. (*The Tozer
Pulpit*, Book. 8, p. 81)

Mystery always baffles the understanding and
stuns the mind, and we come before God in
speechless humility in the presence of the mystery
inexpressible. I feel that we should always leave
room for mystery in our Christian faith. When we
do not, we become evangelical rationalists and we
can explain everything. Just ask us any question
and we're quick on the trigger—we can answer
the question. I don't believe that we can. I think
mystery runs throughout all the kingdom of God
just as there is mystery running throughout nature. And the wisest and most honest scientist will
tell you that he knows practically nothing. And
the Christian who has met God and seen God on
His throne with the eyes of his heart has stopped
being an oracle. He won't pretend to know everything any more and he also won't condemn an-

other man who might take a little different position from his. (Sermon, "The Man Who Saw God," Wheaton College, 1961)

You can have all the plans you want and you can get the help from all the advertisers and you can get the help of modern mechanical gadgets, and when it's all done you will fall short unless first God is glorified in the midst of His Church. (Sermon, "Babylonian Captivity," General Council, 1960)

In worship several elements may be distinguished, among them love, admiration, wonder and adoration. Though they may not be experienced in that order, a little thought will reveal those elements as being present wherever true worship is found. (*That Incredible Christian*. p. 126)

God dwells in the heart where praise is. Man is made to admire something, and he admires. And when he admires to the point of incandescent white heat charged with mystery, that's worship. The world has made a mistake. Some people admire everything, some admire nothing and some admire the wrong things, but God has given us Himself and says, "Here, admire Me, I am God." (Last sermon at Chicago, 1959)

Chapter 3

Unacceptable Worship

What Is Not Acceptable?

The stark, tragic fact is that the efforts of many people to worship are unacceptable to God. Without an infusion of the Holy Spirit there can be no true worship. This is serious. It is hard for me to rest peacefully at night knowing that millions of cultured, religious people are merely carrying on church traditions and religious customs and they are not actually reaching God at all. (*Whatever Happened to Worship?*, p. 46)

The manner in which many moderns think about worship makes me uncomfortable. Can true worship be engineered and manipulated? Do you foresee with me the time to come when churches may call the pastor a "spiritual engineer?" (*Whatever Happened to Worship?*, p. 85)

You are not worshiping God as you should if you have departmentalized your life so that some areas worship and other parts do not worship.

This can be a great delusion—that worship only happens in church or in the midst of a dangerous storm or in the presence of some unusual and sublime beauty of nature around us. I have been with some fellows who became very spiritual when they stood on the breathtaking curve of a steep mountain cliff! (*Whatever Happened to Worship?* p, 124)

It is impossible for any of us to worship God without the impartation of the Holy Spirit. It is the operation of the Spirit of God within us that enables us to worship God acceptably through that Person we call Jesus Christ, who is Himself God.

So worship originates with God and comes back to us and is reflected from us, as a mirror. God accepts no other kind of worship. (*Whatever Happened to Worship?*, pp. 44-45)

I can offer no worship wholly pleasing to God if I know that I am harboring elements in my life that are displeasing to Him. I cannot truly and joyfully worship God on Sunday and not worship Him on Monday. I cannot worship God with a glad song on Sunday and then knowingly displease Him in my business dealings on Monday and Tuesday.

I repeat my view of worship—*no worship is wholly pleasing to God until there is nothing in me dis-*

pleasing to God. (Whatever Happened to Worship?
pp. 124-125)

Lessons from Cain

There are many kinds of worship that God cannot accept. Cain's worship in the Old Testament
was not accepted because he did not acknowledge
the necessity of an atonement for sin in the relationship between God and fallen man. (*Whatever
Happened to Worship?*, p. 40)

The kind of worship Cain offered to God has
three basic and serious shortcomings.

First is the mistaken idea that God is a different
kind of God than what He really is. This has to
do with the person and the character of the sovereign and holy God. How can anyone ever worship
God acceptably without knowing what kind of
God He really is? Cain surely did not know the
true character of God. Cain did not believe that
the matter of man's sin was eternally important to
God.

Second is the mistake of thinking that man
holds a relationship to God that in fact he does
not. Cain casually assumed that he was deserv-
ing of acceptance by the Lord without an inter-
mediary. He refused to accept the judgment of
God that man had been alienated from his God
by sin.

Third, Cain in the Old Testament record, and
with him an unnumbered multitude of men and
women since, have mistakenly assumed that sin is

far less serious than it really is. The record is plain, if men and women would only look at it and consider it. God hates sin because He is a holy God. He knows that sin has filled the world with pain and sorrow, robbing us of our principle purpose and joy in life, the joy of worshiping our God!

The kind of worship offered by Cain is inadequate, without real meaning. Bringing it as an issue to our own day under the New Testament, I assure you that I would not knowingly spend an hour in any church that refuses to teach the necessity of the blood atonement for sin through the cross and the merits of the death of our Lord Jesus Christ! (*Whatever Happened to Worship?*, pp. 41-42)

Emptiness of the Average Church Service

It will be seen how empty and meaningless is the average church service today. All the means are in evidence; the one ominous weakness is the absence of the Spirit's power. The form of godliness is there, and often the form is perfected till it is an aesthetic triumph. Music and poetry, art and oratory, symbolic vesture and solemn tones combine to charm the mind of the worshiper, but too often the supernatural afflatus is not there. The power from on high is neither known nor desired by pastor or people. This is nothing less than tragic, and all the more so because it falls within the field of religion where the eternal destinies of men are involved. (*God's Pursuit of Man*, [previously titled *The Divine Conquest* and *The Pursuit of Man*], p. 90)

The Whole Life Must Worship God

It is possible to worship God with our lips and not worship God with our lives. But I want to tell you that if your life doesn't worship God, your lips don't worship God either. (Sermon, "Doctrine of the Remnant," Chicago, 1957)

Tozer's Convictions

The total life, the whole man and the whole woman, has got to worship God. Faith and love and obedience and loyalty and conduct and life—all of these are to worship God. If there is anything in you that doesn't worship God, then there isn't anything in you that does worship God very well. If you departmentalize your life and let certain parts of you worship God but other parts of you do not worship God, you are not worshiping God as you should. It is a great delusion that we easily fall into the idea that in church or in the presence of death or in the midst of sublimity that we are spiritual. ("The Chief End of Man," Sermon #6, Toronto, 1962)

There is Samaritan worship. Samaritan worship is heretical worship in the correct meaning of the term. A heretic is not a man who denies all of the truth, he's just a very persnickety man who picks out what he likes and rejects the rest. Heresy means I take what I like and I reject what I don't like. ("The Chief End of Man," Sermon #3, Toronto, 1962)

There is nature worship. It is the poetry of religion. It is the high enjoyment and the contemplation of the sublime. We have an awful lot of nature worshipers and worshipers of God through nature, which is a better way of saying it. It is a high enjoyment, a concentrating of the mind upon beauty as distinct from the eye and the ear. If your ear hears music, that's beauty. If your eye sees beauty, that's art. But if you think beautiful thoughts without music or art, that's poetry and you write that down. Some people mistake rapt feeling for worship. ("The Chief End of Man," Sermon #3, Toronto, 1962)

Some mistake the music of religion for worship. Whatever elevates the mind and raises to near rapture the soul, that's supposed to be worship. (The Chief End of Man, Sermon #3, Toronto, 1962)

Not all worship is acceptable with God. And there is a lot of worship in our cultured society that God will never receive in this world or the next. There is religious experience that God will never accept. There is the warm feeling of personal friendships with religious people. There is the sound of the organ and the beauty of the hymns. But apart from truth and the Holy Ghost there is no true worship. ("The Chief End of Man," Sermon #3, Toronto, 1962)

You cannot worship just as you please. This is one of the tricks of the devil and a very favorite pet of unconverted poets and unconverted people with a bump of sublimity on their head but without the new birth. They teach that we just worship God any way we want to worship God and all will be well. Authentic religious experience is altogether possible apart from redemption. It's entirely possible to have authentic religious experience and not be a Christian and not be converted and be on our way to eternal hell. You remember that Cain had an experience—an authentic religious experience. He talked to God and God talked to him. It is possible to have an experience with God and yet not have a saving experience with God. It is possible to worship and yet not worship aright. ("The Chief End of Man," Sermon #3, Toronto, 1962)

Worship has to be in the Spirit and by the Spirit. The notion that just anybody can worship is all wrong. The notion that we can worship without the Spirit is all wrong. The notion that we can crowd the Spirit into a corner and ignore Him, quench Him, resist Him and yet worship God acceptably is a great heresy which we need to correct. Only the Holy Spirit knows how to worship God acceptably. ("The Chief End of Man," Sermon #8, Toronto, 1962)

Worship Comes Before Work

It may be set down as an axiom that if we do not worship we cannot work acceptably. The Holy Spirit can work through a worshiping heart and through no other kind. We may go through the motions and delude ourselves by our religious activity, but we are setting ourselves up for a shocking disillusionment some day.

Without doubt the emphasis in Christian teaching today should be on worship. There is little danger that we shall become merely worshipers and neglect the practical implications of the gospel. No one can long worship God in spirit and in truth before the obligation to holy service becomes too strong to resist. Fellowship with God leads straight to obedience and good works. That is the divine order and it can never be reversed. (*Born after Midnight*, pp. 125-126)

Whatever keeps me from the Bible is my enemy, however harmless it may appear to be. Whatever engages my attention when I should be meditating on God and things eternal does injury to my soul. Let the cares of life crowd out the Scriptures from my mind and I have suffered loss where I can least afford it. Let me accept anything else instead of the Scriptures and I have been cheated and robbed to my eternal confusion. (*That Incredible Christian*, p. 82)

A Hard Message

If there is anything in me that does not worship God, then there is nothing in me that worships God perfectly!

I do not say that God must have a perfection of worship or He will not accept any worship at all.

I would not go so far; if I did, I would rule myself out. And we would all hang our harps on the willows and refuse to sing the songs of the Lord in a strange land.

But, I do say that the ideal God sets before us is that we should worship as near to perfectly as we can. And that if there are areas in my being that are not harmonious and that do not worship God, then there's no area in my being that worships God perfectly. *(The Tozer Pulpit,* Book 1, p. 55)

See to it that there isn't a spot or an hour or a place or a time or a day or a location that isn't consecrated and given over to God. You'll be worshiping Him—and He'll accept it! *(The Tozer Pulpit,* Book 1, p. 53)

Chapter 4

Spiritual Concentration

Accenting the Inner Life

R etire from the world each day to some private spot, even if it be only the bedroom (for a while I retreated to the furnace room for want of a better place). Stay in the secret place till the surrounding noises begin to fade out of your heart and a sense of God's presence envelops you. Deliberately tune out the unpleasant sounds and come out of your closet determined not to hear them. Listen for the inward Voice till you learn to recognize it. Stop trying to compete with others. Give yourself to God and then be what and who you are without regard to what others think. Reduce your interests to a few. . . . Learn to pray inwardly every moment. After a while you can do this even while you work. Practice candor, childlike honesty, humility. Pray for a single eye. Read less, but read more of what is important to your inner life. Never let your mind remain scattered for very long. Call home your roving thoughts. Gaze on Christ with the eyes of your soul. Practice spiritual concentration. (*Of God and Men*, p. 106)

Let's practice the art of Bible meditation. But please don't grab that phrase and go out and form a club—we are organized to death already. Just meditate. Let us just be plain, thoughtful Christians. Let us open our Bibles, spread them out on a chair and meditate on the Word of God. It will open itself to us, and the Spirit of God will come and brood over it.

I do challenge you to meditate, quietly, reverently, prayerfully, for a month. Put away questions and answers and the filling in of blank lines in the portions you haven't been able to understand. Put all of the cheap trash away and take the Bible, get on your knees, and in faith, say, "Father, here I am. Begin to teach me!" (*The Tozer Pulpit*, Book 2, p. 117)

Consecration Is Not Difficult

Consecration is not difficult for the person who has met God. Where there is genuine adoration and fascination, God's child wants nothing more than the opportunity to pour out his or her love at the Savior's feet. (*Whatever Happened to Worship?*, p. 89)

Unhealthy Attitudes

The amount of loafing practiced by the average Christian in spiritual things would ruin a concert pianist if he allowed himself to do the same thing in the field of music. The idle puttering around that we see in church circles would end the career of a big league pitcher in one week. No scientist could solve his exacting problem if he took as little interest in it as the rank and file of Christians take in the art of being holy. The nation whose soldiers were as soft and undisciplined as the soldiers of the churches would be conquered by the first enemy that attacked it. Triumphs are not won by men in easy chairs. Success is costly.

If we would progress spiritually, we must separate ourselves unto the things of God and concentrate upon them to the exclusion of a thousand things the worldly man considers important. (*We Travel an Appointed Way*, pp. 26-27)

Critique of Meaningless Activity

Our religious activities should be ordered in such a way as to leave plenty of time for the cultivation of the fruits of solitude and silence. It should be remembered, however, that it is possible to waste such quiet periods as we may be able to snatch for ourselves out of the clamorous day. Our meditation must be directed toward God; otherwise, we may spend our time of retinal in quiet converse with ourselves. This may quiet our nerves but will not further our spiritual life in any way. (*That Incredible Christian*, p. 137)

Let a Christian insist upon rising above the poor average of current religious experience and

he will soon come up against the need to know
God Himself as the ultimate goal of all Christian
doctrine. Let him seek to explore the sacred wonders of the Triune Godhead and he will discover
that sustained and intelligently directed meditation on the Person of God is imperative. To know
God well he must think on Him unceasingly.
Nothing that man has discovered about himself or
God has revealed any shortcut to pure spirituality.
It is still free, but tremendously costly. (*That Incredible Christian*, p. 135)

Neglected Christian truths can be revitalized
only when by prayer and long meditation we iso-
late them from the mass of hazy ideas with which
our minds are filled and hold them steadily and
determinedly in the focus of the mind's attention.
(*God's Pursuit of Man*, p. 20)

Gazing on God

When we lift our inward eyes to gaze upon
God we are sure to meet friendly eyes gazing back
at us, for it is written that the eyes of the Lord run
to and fro throughout all the earth. The sweet language of experience is "Thou God seen me" (Genesis 16:13). When the eyes of the soul looking out
meet the eyes of God looking in, heaven has be-
gun right here on this earth. (*The Pursuit of God*, p.
83)

Looking is of the heart and can be done successfully by any man standing up or kneeling down or

lying in his last agony a thousand miles from any church. (*The Pursuit of God*, p. 85)

Many have found the secret of which I speak and, without giving much thought to what is going on within them, constantly practice this habit of inwardly gazing upon God. They know that something inside their hearts sees God. Even when they are compelled to withdraw their conscious attention in order to engage in earthly affairs, there is within them a secret communion always going on. Let their attention but be released for a moment from necessary business and it flies at once to God again. This has been the testimony of many Christians, so many that even as I state it thus I have a feeling that I am quoting, though from whom or from how many I cannot possibly know. (*The Pursuit of God*, p. 86)

Private prayer should be practiced by every Christian. Long periods of Bible meditation will purify our gaze and direct it; church attendance will enlarge our outlook and increase our love for others. Service and work and activity—all are good and should be engaged in by every Christian. But at the bottom of all these things, giving meaning to them, will be the inward habit of beholding God. A new set of eyes (so to speak) will develop within us enabling us to be looking at God while our outward eyes are seeing the scenes of this passing world. (*The Pursuit of God*, p. 87)

I would emphasize this one committal, this one great volitional act which establishes the heart's intention to gaze forever upon Jesus. God takes this intention for our choice and makes what allowances He must for the thousand distractions which beset us in this evil world. He knows that we have set the direction of our hearts toward Jesus, and we can know it too, and comfort ourselves with the knowledge that a habit of soul is forming which will become, after a while, a sort of spiritual reflex requiring no more conscious effort on our part. (*The Pursuit of God*, p. 82)

The Voice of God

When God spoke out of heaven to our Lord, self-centered men who heard it explained it by natural causes, saying, "It thundered." This habit of explaining the Voice by appeals to natural law is at the very root of modern science. In the living, breathing cosmos there is a mysterious Something, too wonderful, too awful for any mind to understand. The believing man does not claim to understand. He falls to his knees and whispers, "God!" The man of earth kneels also, but not to worship. He kneels to examine, to search, to find the cause and the how of things. Just now we happen to be living in a secular age. Our thought habits are those of the scientist, not those of the worshiper. We are more likely to explain than to adore. "It thundered!" we exclaim, and go our earthly way. But still the Voice sounds and searches. The order and life of the world depend upon that Voice, but men are mostly too busy or too stubborn to give attention. (*The Pursuit of God*, p. 71)

Safety in Silence

Whoever will listen will hear the speaking Heaven. This is definitely not the hour when men take kindly to an exhortation to listen, for listening is not today a part of popular religion. We are at the opposite end of the pole from there. Religion has accepted the monstrous heresy that noise, size, activity and bluster make a man dear to God. But we may take heart. To a people caught in the tempest of the last great conflict God says, "Be still, and know that I am God" (Psalm 46:10), and still He says it, as if He means to tell us that our strength and safety lie not in noise but in silence. (*The Pursuit of God*, p. 74)

Chapter 5

The Presence of God

Important to Christian Experience

The presence of the Lord is the most wonderful thing in all the world. ("The Chief End of Man," Sermon #4, Toronto, 1962)

We must be convinced to the point where we can go into the presence of God in absolute confidence and say, "Let God be true and every man a liar." When we can do this in the presence of God we are at the beginnings of worship. ("The Chief End of Man," Sermon #5, Toronto, 1962)

We must rescue our own concepts, not rescue God. God needs no rescuers. But we must rescue our own concepts from their fallen and frightfully inadequate condition. ("The Chief End of Man," Sermon #5, Toronto, 1962)

There comes the love of excellence that you can go into the presence of God and not want to rush out again. You want to stay in the presence of God because you are in the presence of utter, infinite excellence. And so naturally, you would admire. This can grow on you until your heart is lifted into an excellency of love and admiration. ("The Chief End of Man," Sermon #5, Toronto, 1962)

If you do not know the presence of God in your office, your factory, your home, then God is not in the church when you attend. (*Whatever Happened to Worship?*, p. 123)

What the Church needs today is a restoration of the vision of the Most High God. I'm not just making up a sermon to preach to you. This is sound and can be checked and tested and proved. What we need more than we need anything else is a restoration of the vision of the Most High God. The honor of God has been lost to men and the God of today's Christianity is a weakling—a little cheap, palsy God that you can run and pal around with. He's "the man upstairs." He's the fellow that can help you when you're in difficulty and not bother you too much when you're not. We've reduced the God of Abraham and Jacob to a stuffed God that can be appealed to by anybody at any time. The clown on the radio can break into his fun and say, "Now we will have a minute of prayer." The half-converted cowboy dressed like an idiot will say after he's twanged out some

sexy numbers, "Now I'll do you a holy number."
God is approached by everybody because that
kind of God can be approached by anybody.
We've lost the glory and honor of God. (Sermon,
"Prayer," Chicago, 1956)

Examples from History

The spiritual giants of old were men who at
some time became acutely conscious of the real
Presence of God and maintained that consciousness for the rest of their lives. The first encounter
may have been one of terror, as when a "horror of
great darkness" fell upon Abram, or as when Moses at the bush hid his face because he was afraid
to look upon God. Usually this fear soon lost its
content of terror and changed after a while to delight some awe, to level off finally into a reverent
sense of complete nearness to God. The essential
point is, *they experienced God.* How otherwise can
the saints and prophets be explained? How otherwise can we account for the amazing power for
good they have exercised over countless generations? Is it not that they walked in conscious communion with the real Presence and addressed
their prayers to God with the artless conviction
that they were addressing Someone actually
there? (*God's Pursuit of Man*, pp. 26-27)

Our fathers have told us and our own hearts
confirm how wonderful is this sense of Someone
there. It makes religion invulnerable to critical
attack. It secures the mind against collapse under

the battering of the enemy. They who worship the God who is present may ignore the objections of unbelieving men. Their experience is self-verifying and needs neither defense nor proof. What they see and hear overwhelms their doubts and confirms their assurance beyond the power of argument to destroy. (*God's Pursuit of Man*, pp. 24-25)

Essential Experience

Whatever else it embraces, true Christian experience must always include a genuine encounter with God. Without this, religion is but a shadow, a reflection of reality, a cheap copy of an original once enjoyed by someone else of whom we have heard. It cannot but be a major tragedy in the life of any man to live in a church from childhood to old age with nothing more real than some synthetic god compounded of theology and logic, but having no eyes to see, no ears to hear and no heart to love. (*God's Pursuit of Man*, p. 26)

The believing man is overwhelmed suddenly by a powerful feeling that only God matters; soon this works itself out into his mental life and conditions all his judgments and all his values. Now he finds himself free from slavery to man's opinions. A mighty desire to please only God lays hold of him. Soon he learns to love above all else the assurance that he is well pleasing to the Father in heaven. (*God's Pursuit of Man*, p. 42)

Trust the Spirit

In coming to God we should place ourselves in
His presence with the confidence that He is the
aggressor, not we. He has been waiting to manifest Himself to us till such time as our noise and
activity have subsided enough for Him to make
Himself heard and felt by us. Then we should focus our soul's powers of attention upon the Triune Godhead. Whether One Person or another
claims our present interest is not important. We
can trust the Spirit to bring before our minds the
Person that we at the moment need most to behold. (*That Incredible Christian*, p. 137)

Illustrated in the Tabernacle

The interior journey of the soul from the wilds
of sin into the enjoyed presence of God is beautifully illustrated in the Old Testament tabernacle.
The returning sinner first entered the outer court
where he offered a blood sacrifice on the brazen
altar and washed himself in the laver that stood
near it. Then he passed through a veil into the
holy place where no natural light could come, but
the golden candlestick which spoke of Jesus, the
Light of the World, threw its soft glow over all.
There also was the shewbread to tell of Jesus, the
Bread of Life, and the altar of incense, a figure of
unceasing prayer.

Though the worshiper had enjoyed so much,
still he had not yet entered the presence of God.
Another veil separated from the Holy of Holies

where above the mercy seat dwelt the very God Himself in awful and glorious manifestation. While the tabernacle stood, only the high priest could enter there, and that but once a year, with blood which he offered for his sins and the sins of the people. It was this last veil which was rent when our Lord gave up the ghost on Calvary, and the sacred writer explains that this rending of the veil opened the way for every worshiper in the world to come by the new and living way straight into the divine Presence. (*The Pursuit of God*, pp. 33-34)

A Loving Personality

Over against all this cloudy vagueness stands the clear scriptural doctrine that God can be known in personal experience. A loving Personality dominates the Bible, walking among the trees of the garden and breathing fragrance over every scene. Always a living Person is present, speaking, pleading, loving, working and manifesting Himself whenever and wherever His people have the receptivity necessary to receive the manifestation. (*The Pursuit of God*, p. 46)

God-Consciousness

As we begin to focus upon God, the things of the spirit will take shape before our inner eyes. Obedience to the word of Christ will bring an inward revelation of the Godhead (John 14:21-23). It will give acute perception enabling us to see God even as is promised to the pure in heart. A new God-consciousness will seize upon us and we shall begin to taste and hear and inwardly feel God, who is our life and our all. There will be seen the constant shining of "the true Light, which lighteth every man that cometh into the world" (John 1:9). More and more, as our faculties grow sharper and more sure, God will become to us the great All, and His presence the glory and wonder of our lives. (*The Pursuit of God*, p. 54)

An Important Distinction

The Presence and the manifestation of the Presence are not the same. There can be the one without the other. God is here when we are wholly without the other. God is here when we are wholly unaware of it. He is manifest only when and as we are aware of His presence. On our part, there must be surrender to the Spirit of God, for His work is to show us the Father and the Son. If we cooperate with Him in loving obedience, God will manifest Himself to us, and that manifestation will be the difference between a nominal Christian life and a life radiant with the light of His face. (*The Pursuit of God*, p. 58)

God's Presence Is Fact

The universal Presence is a fact. God is here. The whole universe is alive with His life. And He is no strange or foreign God, but the familiar Father of our Lord Jesus Christ whose love has for these thousands of years enfolded the sinful race of men. And always He is trying to get our attention to reveal Himself to us, to communicate with us. We have within us the ability to know Him if we will but respond to His overtures. (And this we call pursuing God!) We will know Him in increasing degree as our receptivity becomes more perfect by faith and love and practice. (*The Pursuit of God*, p. 64)

Similarly the presence of God is the central fact of Christianity. At the heart of the Christian message is God Himself waiting for His redeemed children to push in to conscious awareness of His presence. That type of Christianity which happens now to be the vogue knows this Presence only in theory. It fails to stress the Christian's privilege of present realization. According to its teachings we are in the presence of God positionally, and nothing is said about the need to experience that Presence actually. The fiery urge that drove men like McCheyne is wholly missing. And the present generation of Christians measures itself by this imperfect rule. Ignoble contentment takes the place of burning zeal. We are satisfied to rest in our judicial possessions and for the most part, we bother ourselves very little about the absence of personal experience. (*The Pursuit of God*, p. 35)

It's Often Missing

The presence of God in our midst—bringing a sense of godly fear and reverence—this is largely missing today.

You cannot induce it by soft organ music and light streaming through beautifully designed windows. You cannot induce it by holding up a biscuit and claiming that it is God. You cannot induce it by any kind or any amount of mumbo-jumbo.

What people feel in the presence of that kind of paganism is not the true fear of God. It is just the inducement of a superstitious dread.

A true fear of God is a beautiful thing, for it is worship, it is love, it is veneration. It is a high moral happiness because God is. It is a delight so great that if God were not, the worshiper would not want to be, either. He or she could easily pray, "My God, continue to be as Thou art, or let me die! I cannot think of any other God but Thee!"

True worship is to be so personally and hopelessly in love with God that the idea of a transfer of affection never even remotely exists. (*Whatever Happened to Worship?*, p. 33)

Chapter 6

Personal Communion

Importance for Believers

I believe in personal communion with God to the point of incandescence. And I believe that we should fellowship with God until, like Moses, there is some of the glow of God upon our faces. (Sermon, "The Man Who Exalted God," Wheaton College, 1961)

God Is Easy to Live With

How good it would be if we could learn that God is easy to live with. He remembers our frame and knows that we are dust. He may sometimes chasten us, it is true. But even this He does with a smile, the proud tender smile of a Father who is bursting with pleasure over an imperfect but promising son who is coming every day to look more and more like the One whose child he is. (*The Root of the Righteous*, p. 16)

The fellowship of God is delightful beyond all telling. He communes with His redeemed ones in an easy, uninhibited fellowship that is restful and healing to the soul. He is not sensitive nor selfish nor temperamental. What He is today we shall find Him tomorrow and the next day and the next year. He is not hard to please, though He may be hard to satisfy. He expects of us only what He has Himself first supplied. He is quick to mark every simple effort to please Him and just as quick to overlook imperfections when He knows we meant to do His will. He loves us for ourselves and values our love more than galaxies of new created worlds. (*The Root of the Righteous*, p. 15)

The Reality of Religion

The man who has met God is not looking for something—he has found it; he is not searching for light—upon him the Light has already shined. His certainty may seem bigoted, but his is the assurance of one who knows by experience. His religion is not hearsay; he is not a copy, not a facsimile print; he is an original from the hand of the Holy Ghost. (*The Root of the Righteous*, p. 157)

In the Spirit's Hands

The primary work of the Holy Spirit is to restore the lost soul to intimate fellowship with God through the washing of regeneration. To accomplish this He first reveals Christ to the penitent heart (1 Corinthians 12:3). He then goes on to illumine the newborn soul with brighter rays from the face of Christ (John 14:26; 16:13-15) and leads the willing heart into depths and heights of divine knowledge and communion. Remember, we know Christ only as the Spirit enables us and we have only as much of Him as the Holy Spirit imparts.

God wants worshipers before workers; indeed the only acceptable workers are those who have learned the lost art of worship. It is inconceivable that a sovereign and holy God should be so hard up for workers that He would press into service anyone who had been empowered regardless of his moral qualifications. The very stones would praise Him if the need arose and a thousand legions of angels would leap to do His will.

Gifts and power for service the Spirit surely desires to impart; but holiness and spiritual worship come first. (*That Incredible Christian*, p. 37)

To Know God

To know God it is necessary that we be like God to some degree, for things wholly dissimilar cannot agree and beings wholly unlike can never have communion with each other. It is necessary therefore that we use every means of grace to bring our souls into harmony with the character of God. (*That Incredible Christian*, p. 84)

To enjoy this growing knowledge of God will require that we go beyond the goals so casually set by modern evangelicals. We must fix our hearts on God and purposefully aim to rise above the dead level and average of current Christianity. (*That Incredible Christian*, p. 85)

Perhaps the most serious charge that can be brought against modern Christians is that we are not sufficiently in love with Christ. The Christ of fundamentalism is strong but hardly beautiful. It is rarely that we find anyone aglow with personal love for Christ. I trust it is not uncharitable to say that in my opinion a great deal of praise in conservative circles is perfunctory and forced where it is not downright insincere.

Many of our popular songs and choruses in praise of Christ are hollow and unconvincing. Some are even shocking in their amorous endearments and strike a reverent soul as being a kind of flattery offered to One with whom neither composer nor singer is acquainted. The whole thing is in the mood of the love ditty, the only difference being the substitution of the name of Christ for that of the earthly lover. (*That Incredible Christian*, p. 129)

Freedom in God

The more perfect our friendship with God becomes the simpler will our lives be. Those formalities that are so necessary to keep a casual friendship alive may be dispensed with when true friends sit in each other's presence. True friends trust each other. (*That Incredible Christian*, p. 121)

God is not satisfied until there exists between

Him and His people a relaxed informality that requires no artificial stimulation. The true friend of
God may sit in His presence for long periods in
silence. Complete trust needs no words of assurance. Such words have long ago been spoken and
the adoring heart can safely be still before God.
(*That Incredible Christian*, p. 121)

Christ can never be known without a sense of
awe and fear accompanying the knowledge. He is
the fairest among ten thousand, but He is also the
Lord high and mighty. He is the friend of sinners,
but He is also the terror of devils. He is meek and
lowly in heart, but He is also Lord and Christ who
will surely come to be the Judge of all men. No
one who knows Him intimately can ever be flip-
pant in His presence. (*That Incredible Christian*, p.
129)

God's Purpose in Our Creation

We should never forget that God created us to
be joyful worshipers, but sin drew us into everything else but worship. Then in God's love and
mercy in Christ Jesus, we were restored into the
fellowship of the Godhead through the miracle of
the new birth. (*Whatever Happened to Worship?*, p.
82)

A Sense for God

We have in our hearts organs by means of
which we can know God as certainly as we know
material things through our familiar five senses.

We apprehend the physical world by exercising the faculties given us for that purpose, and we possess spiritual faculties by means of which we can know God and the spiritual world if we will obey the Spirit's urge and begin to use them. (*The Pursuit of God*, p. 47)

Chapter 7

The Power of God in Worship

Tozer's Sentiment

For myself, if I couldn't have the divine power of God, I would quit the whole business. I would walk out and stop the whole business. The church that wants God's power will have something to offer besides social clubs, knitting societies, the Boy Scout troops and all of the other side issues. (*The Tozer Pulpit*, Book 2, p. 12)

Oh, go back into the Word of God and consider how thirsty the friends of God were for God Himself! The great difference between us and Abraham, David and Paul is that they sought Him and found Him and seeking Him still, found Him and sought Him—continually!

We accept Him—and seek Him no more and that is the difference. (*The Tozer Pulpit*, Book 8, p. 85)

Get alone with God and His Word every day. I recommend that you turn off the radio and the television and let your soul delight in the fellowship and the mercies of God. (*The Tozer Pulpit*, Book 6, p. 74)

Worship Is Cultivated

Receptivity is not a single thing; rather, it is a compound, a blending of several elements within the soul. It is an affinity for, a bent toward, a sympathetic response to, a desire to have. From this it may be gathered that it can be present in degrees, that we may have little or more, depending upon the individual. It may be increased by exercise or destroyed by neglect. It is not a sovereign and irresistible force which comes upon us as a seizure from above. It is a gift of God indeed, but one which must be recognized and cultivated as any other gift if we are to realize the purpose for which is was given. (*The Pursuit of God*, p. 62)

Spiritual Longing

Occasionally there will appear on the religious scene a man whose unsatisfied spiritual longings become so big and important in his life that they crowd out every other interest. Such a man refuses to be content with the safe and conventional prayers of the frost-bound brethren who "lead in prayer" week after week and year after year in the local assemblies. His yearnings carry him away and often make something of a nuisance out of him. His puzzled fellow Christians shake their heads and look knowingly at each other. But like the blind man who cried after his sight and was rebuked by the disciples, he "cries the more a great deal." And if he has not yet met the conditions or there is something hindering the answer to his prayer, he may pray on into the late hours. Not the hour of night but the state of his heart decides the time of his visitation. For him it may well be that revival comes after midnight. (*Born after Midnight*, p. 8)

Chapter 8

Adoration

Reverence in Worship

The simple truth is that worship is elementary until it begins to take on the quality of admiration. Just as long as the worshiper is engrossed with himself and his good fortune, he is a babe. We begin to grow up when our worship passes from thanksgiving to admiration. As our hearts rise to God in lofty esteem for that which He is ("I AM THAT I AM"), we begin to share a little of the selfless pleasure which is the portion of the blessed in heaven. (*That Incredible Christian*, p. 127)

There are many great lessons for us in the worship and reverence of the heavenly seraphim Isaiah described in his vision.

I notice that they covered their feet and they covered their faces. Because of the presence of the Holy God, they reverently covered their faces.

Reverence is a beautiful thing, and it is so rare in this terrible day in which we live.

Churches don't really succeed in trying to "induce" reverence. You can't do it with statues and beautiful windows and carpeting on the floor and everyone talking through his adenoids.

But a man who has passed the veil and looked even briefly upon the holy face of Isaiah's God can never be irreverent again.

There will be a reverence in his spirit and instead of boasting, he will cover his feet modestly. (*The Tozer Pulpit*, Book 1, pp. 57-58)

Worship Anywhere

Who needs a bushel basket full of claptrap in order to serve the Lord? You can worship God anywhere if you will let Him work in your being and suffer no rival. You may be still with arthritis so that you can't even get on your knees to pray, but you can look up in your heart, for prayer isn't a matter of getting on your knees. Prayer is the elevation of the heart to God and that is all a man needs to praise, to pray and to worship. (*The Tozer Pulpit*, Book 8, p. 51)

The Mysterious Element in Worship

It is true that for each one there must be a personal encounter with God, and often that encounter takes place in the loneliness and silence of retirement. In that sacred moment there must be only God and the individual soul. The mysterious operation of God in regenerating grace and His further work of the Spirit's anointing are transactions so highly personal that no third party can know or understand what is taking place. (*Born after Midnight*, p. 112)

Vocabularies are formed by many minds over long periods and are capable of expressing whatever the mind is capable of entertaining. But when the heart, on its knees, moves into the awesome Presence and hears with fear and wonder things not lawful to utter, then the mind falls flat. And words, previously its faithful servants, become weak and totally incapable of telling what the heart hears and sees. In that awful moment the worshiper can only cry, "Oh!" And that simple exclamation becomes more eloquent than learned speech and, I have no doubt, is dearer to God than any oratory. (*Born after Midnight*, p. 85)

We Christians should watch lest we lose the "Oh!" from our hearts. There is real danger these days that we shall fall victim to the prophets of poise and the purveyors of tranquility, and our Christianity be reduced to a mere evangelical humanism that is never disturbed about anything nor overcome by any "trances of thought and mountings of the mind." When we become too glib in prayer we are most surely talking to ourselves. When the calm listing of requests and the courteous giving of proper thanks take the place of the burdened prayer that finds utterance difficult we should beware of the next step, for our direc-

tion is surely down whether we know it or not.
(*Born after Midnight*, p. 87)

More Romance than Worship

The influence of the erotic spirit is felt almost
everywhere in evangelical circles. Much of the
singing in certain types of meetings has in it more
of romance than it has of the Holy Ghost. Both
words and music are designed to rouse the libidinous. Christ is courted with a familiarity that reveals a total ignorance of who He is. It is not the
reverent intimacy of the adoring saint but the im-
pudent familiarity of the carnal lover. (*Born after
Midnight*, p. 38)

We Must Be Conquered by God

The experiences of men who walked with God
in olden times agree to teach that the Lord cannot
fully bless a man until He has first conquered
him. The degree of blessing enjoyed by any man
will correspond exactly with the completeness of
God's victory over him. This is a badly neglected
tenet of the Christian's creed, not understood by
many in this self-assured age, but it is nevertheless
of living importance to us all. This spiritual principle is well illustrated in the book of Genesis.
(*God's Pursuit of Man*, p. 53)

The pursuit of God will embrace the labor of
bringing our total personality into conformity to
His. And this not judicially but actually. I do not
here refer to the act of justification by faith in

Christ. I speak of a voluntary exalting of God to His proper station over us and a willing surrender of our whole being to the place of worshipful submission which the Creator-creature circumstance makes proper. (*The Pursuit of God*, p. 94)

We can get a right start only by accepting God as He is and learning to love Him for what He is. As we go on to know Him better, we shall find it a source of unspeakable joy that God is just what He is. Some of the most rapturous moments we know will be those we spend in reverent admiration of the Godhead. In those holy moments the very thought of change in Him will be too painful to endure. (*The Pursuit of God*, p. 93)

We Have Broken with God

God formed us for His pleasure, and so formed us that we, as well as He, can, in divine communion, enjoy the sweet and mysterious mingling of kindred personalities. He meant us to see Him and live with Him and draw our life from His smile. But we have been guilty of that "foul revolt" of which Milton speaks when describing the rebellion of Satan and his hosts. We have broken with God. We have ceased to obey Him or love Him, and in guilt and fear have fled as far as possible from His presence. (*The Pursuit of God*, p. 32)

Intimacy through Testing

The way to deeper knowledge of God is through the lonely valleys of soul poverty and abnegation of all things. The blessed ones who possess the kingdom are they who have repudiated every external thing and have rooted from the heart all sense of possessing. There are the "poor in spirit." They have reached an inward state paralleling the outward circumstances of the common beggar in the streets of Jerusalem. That is what the word "poor" as Christ used it actually means. These blessed poor are no longer slaves to the tyranny of things. They have broken the yoke of the oppressor; and this they have done not by fighting but by surrendering. Though free from all sense of possessing, they yet possess all things. "Theirs is the kingdom of heaven." (*The Pursuit of God*, p. 23)

Tozer Stressed Adoration

Such fascination with God must necessarily have an element of adoration. You may ask me for a definition of adoration in this context. I will say that when we adore God, all of the beautiful ingredients of worship are brought to white, incandescent heat with the fire of the Holy Spirit. To adore God means we love Him with all the powers within us. We love Him with fear and wonder and yearning and awe. (*Whatever Happened to Worship?*, p. 88)

Those who have followed the revelation provided by the Creator God have accepted that God never does anything without a purpose. We do believe, therefore, that God had a noble purpose in mind when He created us. We believe that it was distinctly the will of God that men and women created in His image would desire fellowship with Him above all else.

In His plan, it was to be a perfect fellowship based on adoring worship of the Creator and Sustainer of all things. (*Whatever Happened to Worship?*, p. 51)

God desires to take us deeper into Himself. We will have much to learn in the school of the Spirit.

He wants to lead us on in our love for Him who first loved us. He wants to cultivate within us the adoration and admiration of which He is worthy. He wants to reveal to each of us the blessed element of spiritual fascination in true worship. He wants to teach us the wonder of being filled with moral excitement in our worship, entranced with the knowledge of who God is. He wants us to be astonished at the inconceivable elevation and magnitude and splendor of Almighty God! (*Whatever Happened to Worship?*, p. 26)

This communication, this consciousness is not an end but really an inception. There is the point of reality where we begin our fellowship and friendship and communion with God. But where we stop no man had yet discovered for there is in the mysterious depths of the Triune God neither limit nor end.

When we come into this sweet relationship, we are beginning to learn astonished reverence, breathless adoration, awesome fascination, lofty admiration of the attributes of God and something of the breathless silence that we know when God is near. (*Whatever Happened to Worship?*, p. 30)

Tozer's Concern

In the majority of our meetings there is scarcely a trace of reverent thought, no recognition of the unity of the body, little sense of the divine Presence, no moment of stillness, no solemnity, no wonder, no holy fear. But so often there is a dull or a breezy song leader full of awkward jokes, as well as a chairman announcing each "number" with the old radio continuity patter in an effort to make everything hang together. (*God Tells the Man Who Cares*, p. 12)

Yielding to the Holy Spirit

Where the Holy Spirit is permitted to exercise His full sway in a redeemed heart, the progression is likely to be as follows: First, voluble praise, in speech or prayer or witness. Then, when the crescendo rises beyond the ability of studied speech to express, comes song. When song breaks down under the weight of glory, then comes silence where the soul, held in deep fascination, feels itself blessed with an unutterable beatitude. (*This World: Playground or Battleground?*, p. 42)

The man that will have God's best becomes at once the object of the personal attention of the Holy Spirit. Such a man will not be required to wait for the rest of the church to come alive. He will not be penalized for the failures of his fellow Christians, nor be asked to forego the blessing till his sleepy brethren catch up. God deals with the individual heart as exclusively as if only one existed. (*The Size of the Soul*, p. 15)

A Call to Confession

The critical need in this hour of the church's history is not what it is so often said to be: soul-winning, foreign missions, miracles. These are effects, not causes. The most pressing need just now is that we who call ourselves Christians should frankly acknowledge to each other and to God that we are astray; that we should confess that we are worldly, that our moral standards are low and we are spiritually cold. We need to cease our multitude of unscriptural activities, stop running when and where we have not been sent and cease trying to sanctify carnal projects by professing that we are promoting them "in the name of the Lord" and "for the glory of God." We need to return to the message, methods and objectives of the New Testament. We need boldly and indignantly to cleanse the temple of all that sell cattle in the holy place and overthrow the tables of the moneychangers. And this must be done in our own lives first and then in the churches of whom we are a part. (*The Size of the Soul*, p. 132)

Full Surrender

Once the heart is freed from its contrary impulses, Christ within becomes a wondrous experiential fact. The surrendered heart has no more controversy with God, so He can live in us congenial and uninhibited. Then He thinks His own thoughts in us: thoughts about ourselves, about Himself, about sinners and saints and babes and harlots; thoughts about the church, about sin and judgment and hell and heaven. And He thinks about us and Himself and His love for us and our love for Him; and He woos us to Himself as a bridegroom woos his bride. (*That Incredible Christian*, p. 43)

Music of the Soul

The music of the heart is adoration. The music of heaven is adoration. When we get to heaven we will find that the harpers harping on their harps are just adoring God, nothing more. They are not playing "Sweet Adeline" or "Huckleberry Hill." They are adoring God by harping on their harps. And a Spirit-baptized man will be an adorer of God. (Sermon, "Dead Words," General Council)

I am looking for the fellowship of the burning heart—for men and women of all generations everywhere who love the Savior until adoration becomes the music of their soul until they don't have to be fooled with and entertained and amused. Jesus Christ is everything, all-in-all. (Sermon, "Dead Words," General Council)

Tozer Preached Adoration

Man has got to admire, he's got to fear, he's got

to adore. And if he has lost his ability to adore in his spirit and soar in his heart he will soar in a rocket. He'll get out there somehow. The impulse back of the longing to explore other worlds and ride out into the vast spaces is evidence of something within us. No other creature does it and no other creature wants to do it and no other creature thinks of doing it. ("The Chief End of Man," Sermon #7, Toronto, 1962)

Adoration I keep for the only One who deserves it. In no other presence, before no other being can I kneel in fear and wonder and yearning and awe and feel a sense of possessiveness that cries "Mine, mine." ("The Chief End of Man," Sermon #5, Toronto, 1962)

When we've known God enough and come to have faith in Him, when we have boundless confidence in His character, and when we come to admire Him and love Him for His excellence, when we become magnetized by His beauty and adore Him we will want to pour ourselves out at His feet. We don't have to be urged to do it. The person who has ever really met God will want to come and pour himself out at God's feet. Consecration is not difficult to the person who has met God. He insists upon giving himself to God. ("The Chief End of Man," Sermon #5, Toronto, 1962)

You can have respect for a man and not admire him. It would be remotely possible to have some kind of theological respect for God and yet not admire what you saw, particularly. Or have an inability to admire. But when God made man in His own image He gave him a capability of appreciation. He gave him the ability to appreciate and admire his Creator. ("The Chief End of Man," Sermon #5, Toronto, 1962)

Another ingredient that I find in worship is fascination. Fascination is to be filled with moral excitement. (The Chief End of Man, Sermon #5, Toronto, 1962)

The final ingredient of worship that I would mention is adoration, which is all else brought to white heat and made incandescent with the fire of the Holy Ghost. That is to love with all the powers within us, it is to love with fear and wonder and yearning and awe. ("The Chief End of Man," Sermon #5, Toronto, 1962)

The shepherds were the first to come to Jesus in fear and wonder and praise. The Scriptures say that they came in fear but it was not the fear men fear of impending destruction. It wasn't the fear that superstitious people feel for black cats on Friday. It was a godly fear, the fear that heals the heart. It was a wholesome, healing, reverential fear and wonder. And these shepherds who came set the mood for all that will come through all the years. The Christ at whose feet I could not kneel and wonder is the Christ that I could not worship.

I might pay some dutiful tribute to Him in keeping with the way the Church does but I could not worship if I could not wonder. (Sermon on John 3:16, Mahaffey Camp)

Tozer Grieves in Church Services

There is grief in my spirit when I go into the average church, for we have become a generation rapidly losing all sense of divine sacredness in our worship. Many whom we have raised in our churches no longer think in terms of reverence—which seems to indicate they doubt that God's presence is there. (*Whatever Happened to Worship?*, p. 117)

Adoration Is a Present Reality

Looking at what John wrote, I wonder how so many present-day Christians can consider an hour of worship Sunday morning as adequate adoration of the holy God who created them and then redeemed them back to Himself. I have been at funerals where the presiding minister preached the deceased right into heaven. Yet the earthly life of the departed plainly said that he or she would be bored to tears in a heavenly environment of continuous praise and adoration of God.

This is personal opinion, but I do not think death is going to transform our attitudes and disposition. If in this life we are not really comfortable talking or singing about heaven, I doubt that death will transform us into enthusiasts. If the worship and adoration of God are tedious now, they will be tedious after the hour of death. I do not know that God is going to force any of us into His heaven. I doubt that He will say to any of us, "You were never interested in worshiping Me while you were on earth, but in heaven I am going to make that your greatest interest and your ceaseless occupation!" (*Jesus Is Victor*, p. 68)

Called to Flame

Christian believers are called to be burning bushes. They are not necessarily called to be great, or to be promoters and organizers. But they are called to be people in whom the beautifying fire of God dwells, people who have met God in the purifying crisis of encounter! (*Men Who Met God*, p. 77)

Tozer as a Mystic

I get accused occasionally by some of these hard-edged theologians of being a mystic, which I don't deny. A mystic is simply somebody who believes it is possible to commune with God Almighty right now through Jesus Christ in the Spirit and know it and have a sense of heaven all around him and being in the presence of God even when he's in the presence of men. If that's being a mystic then I plead guilty and I am. (Sermon, "Reformation," Chicago)

The word "mystic" . . . refers to that personal spiritual experience common to the saints of Bible times and well known to multitudes of persons in the postbiblical era. I refer to the evangelical mystic who has been brought by the gospel into intimate fellowship with the Godhead. His theology is no less and no more than is taught in the Christian Scriptures. He walks the high road of truth where walked of old prophets and apostles, and where down the centuries walked martyrs, reformers, Puritans, evangelists and missionaries of the cross. He differs from the ordinary orthodox Christian only because he experiences his faith down in the depths of his sentient being while the other does not. He exists in a world of spiritual reality. He is quietly, deeply and sometimes almost ecstatically aware of the presence of God in his own nature and in the world around him. His religious experience is something elemental, as old as time and the creation. It is immediate acquaintance with God by union with the Eternal Son. It is to know that which passes knowledge. (*The Christian Book of Mystical Verse*, p. vi)

Chapter 9

Thoughts of God

God Is a Person

The modern scientist has lost God amid the wonders of His world; we Christians are in real danger of losing God amid the wonders of His Word. We have almost forgotten that God is a person and, as such, can be cultivated as any person can. It is inherent in personality to be able to know other personalities, but full knowledge of one personality by another cannot be achieved in one encounter. It is only after long and loving mental intercourse that the full possibilities of both can be explored. (*The Pursuit of God*, p. 13)

God Is Seeking Man

Our pursuit of God is successful just because He is forever seeking to manifest Himself to us. The revelation of God to any man is not God coming from a distance once upon a time to pay a brief and momentous visit to the man's soul. Thus to think of it is to misunderstand it all. The approach of God to the soul or of the soul to God is not to be thought of in spatial terms at all. There is no idea of physical distance involved in the concept. It is not a matter of miles but of experience. (*The Pursuit of God*, p. 59)

Follow Godly Examples

In my creature impatience I am often caused to wish there were some way to bring modern Christians into a deeper spiritual life painlessly by short easy lessons; but such wishes are vain. No shortcut exists. God has not bowed to our nervous haste nor embraced the methods of our machine age. It is well that we accept the hard truth now: The man who would know God must give time to Him. He must count no time wasted which is spent in the cultivation of His acquaintance. He must give himself to meditation and prayer hours on end. So did the saints of old, the glorious company of the apostles, the goodly fellowship of the prophets and the believing members of the holy Church in all generations. And so must we if we would follow in their train. (*God's Pursuit of Man*, p. 22)

Joy from the Inner Witness

The efforts of some of our teachers to cheer up our drooping spirits are futile because those same teachers reject the very phenomenon that would naturally produce joy, namely, the inner witness.

In their strange fear of the religious emotions they have explained away Scriptures that teach this witness, such as, "The Spirit himself beareth witness" and "He that believeth on the Son of God hath the witness in himself." (*Born after Midnight*, p. 13)

Need of the Spirit's Power

I think there can be no doubt that the need above all other needs in the Church of God at this moment is the power of the Holy Spirit. More education, better organization, finer equipment, more advanced methods—all are unavailing. It is like bringing a better respirator after the patient is dead. Good as these things are, they can never give life. "It is the Spirit that quickeneth." Good as they are they can never bring power. "Power belongeth unto God." Protestantism is on the wrong road when it tries to win merely by means of a "united front." It is not organizational unity we need most; the great need is power. The headstones in the cemetery present a united front, but they stand mute and helpless while the world passes by. (*God's Pursuit of Man*, p. 92)

It is totally impossible to worship God acceptably apart from the Holy Ghost. The operation of the Spirit of God within us enables us to worship God acceptably through that person we call Jesus Christ, who is Himself God. Worship originates with God and comes back to us and is reflected from us as a mirror. ("The Chief End of Man," Sermon #3, Toronto, 1962)

Revival

What does happen, then, in a Christian church when a fresh and vital working of the Spirit of God brings revival? In my study and observations, a revival generally results in a sudden bestowment of a spirit of worship. This is not the result of engineering or of manipulation. It is something God bestows on people hungering and thirsting for Him. With spiritual renewing will come a blessed spirit of loving worship.

These believers worship gladly because they have a high view of God. In some circles, God has been abridged, reduced, modified, edited, changed and amended until He is no longer the God whom Isaiah saw, high and lifted up. Because He has been reduced in the minds of so many people, we no longer have that boundless confidence in His character that we used to have. (*Whatever Happened to Worship?*, p. 86)

Revival would be nothing less than the sudden coming down of the Holy Ghost upon the people and taking their eyes off of themselves and putting their eyes on the Son of God. ("The Chief End of Man," Sermon #9, Toronto, 1962)

Chapter 10

Hymns

Joining the Author in Worship

A great hymn embodies the purest concentrated thoughts of some lofty saint who may have long ago gone from the earth and left little or nothing behind except that hymn. To read or sing a true hymn is to join in the act of worship with a great and gifted soul in his moments of intimate devotion. It is to hear a lover of Christ explaining to his Savior why he loves Him; it is to listen in without embarrassment on the softest whisperings of undying love between the bride and the heavenly Bridegroom. (*We Travel an Appointed Way*, p. 64)

Those of you who have gone on to read the great books of devotion within the Christian faith know, too, that this yearning for perfection was the temper of all the superior souls who have ever lived. They have written our great works of faith and love and devotion and they have composed our loftiest hymns. It is to our shame that we as unworthy spiritual descendants of those great fathers so often use their hymns without any spiritual awareness of what we are singing! (*The Tozer Pulpit*, Book 8, p. 11)

To Celebrate Truth

Hymns do not create truth, nor even reveal it; they celebrate it. They are the response of the trusting heart to a truth revealed or a fact accomplished. God does it and man sings it. God speaks and a hymn is the musical echo of His voice. (*Warfare of the Spirit*, p. 63)

Tozer's Appreciation of Hymns

The hymns came out of this sense of admiration and fascination that was in the hearts of men. The hymnist admired God until he was charmed and struck with wonder at the inconceivable elevation and magnitude and moral splendor of the Being we call God. ("The Chief End of Man," Sermon #5, Toronto, 1962)

I'd rather worship God than any other thing in all the world. I have hymnbooks piled up in my study, and I can't sing a lick but that's nobody's business. God thinks I'm an opera star. He listens while I sing to Him the old hymns and the beautiful psalms done in meter as well as some of the simpler songs of Watts and Wesley and the rest. ("The Chief End of Man, " Sermon # 4, Toronto, 1962)

The devil has a sense of humor, I think. He must laugh and hold his sooty sides when he sees a bunch of dead Christians sing a hymn written by a live composer of sometime or another. ("The Chief End of Man," Sermon #4, Toronto, 1962)

Not Just for the Music

We can come and sing hymns in this church and only enjoy the dignity of the music as a relief from rock-n-roll. (Sermon, "Doctrine of the Remnant," Chicago, 1957)

A Downward Trend

Religious music has long ago fallen victim to this weak and twisted philosophy of godliness. Good hymnody has been betrayed and subverted by noisy, uncouth persons who have too long operated under the immunity afforded them by the timidity of the saints. The tragic result is that for one entire generation we have been rearing Christians who are in complete ignorance of the golden treasury of songs and hymns left us by the ages. The tin horn has been substituted for the silver trumpet, and our religious leaders have been afraid to protest.

It is ironic that the modernistic churches which deny the theology of the great hymns nevertheless sing them, and regenerated Christians who believe them are yet not singing them; in their stead are songs without theological content set to music without beauty.

Not our religious literature only and our hymnody have suffered from the notion that love to be true to itself must be silent in the presence of any and every abomination, but almost every phase of our church life has suffered also. Once a Bible and a hymnbook were enough to allow gospel Christians to express their joy in the public assembly, but now it requires tons of gadgets to satisfy the pagan appetites of persons who call themselves Christians. (*The Size of the Soul*, pp. 189-190)

I'm always suspicious when we talk too much about ourselves. Somebody pointed out that hymnody took a downward trend when we left the great objective hymns that talked about God and began to sing the gospel songs that talk about us. There was a day when men sang "Holy, Holy, Holy," and "O Worship the King," and they talked objectively about the greatness of God. Then we backslide into that gutter where we still are where everything is about "I." "I'm so happy," "I'm so blest," "I'm so nice," "I'm so good," always "I." The difference between heaven and hell is the difference between God and I. Jesus Christ, by canceling His "I" was the Christ of God, not as I will, but as Thou wilt. The devil by magnifying his "I" became the devil—when he said, "I will arise, I will raise my throne above the throne of God." (Sermon, "Ezekiel")

Doctrine Influences Hymnody

Hymnody is sweet with the longing after God, the God whom, while the singer seeks, he knows he has already found. "His track I see and I'll pursue," sang our fathers only a short generation ago, but that song is heard no more in the great congregation. How tragic that we in this dark day have had our seeking done for us by our teachers. Everything is made to center upon the initial act of "accepting" Christ (a term, incidentally, which is not found in the Bible) and we are not expected thereafter to crave any further revelation of God to our souls. We have been snared in the coils of a spurious logic which insists that if we have found Him, we need no more seek Him. This is set before us as the last word in orthodoxy, and it is taken for granted that no Bible-taught Christian ever believed otherwise. Thus the whole testimony of the worshiping, seeking, singing church on that subject is crisply set aside. The experiential heart-theology of a grand army of fragrant saints is rejected in favor of a smug interpretation of Scripture which would certainly have sounded strange to an Augustine, a Rutherford or a Brainerd. (*The Pursuit of God*, p. 16)

Chapter 11

Entertainment:
An Evangelical Heresy

The Anathema of Entertainment

In our day we must be dramatic about everything. We don't want God to work unless He can make a theatrical production of it. We want Him to come dressed in costumes with a beard and with a staff. We want Him to play a part according to our ideas. Some of us even demand that He provide a colorful setting and fireworks as well! (*The Tozer Pulpit*, Book 8, pp. 48-49)

Then there are some among us these days who have to depend upon truckloads of gadgets to get their religion going, and I am tempted to ask: What will they do when they don't have the help of the trappings and gadgets? The truck can't come along where they are going! (*The Tozer Pulpit*, Book 8, p. 50)

Schleiermacher held that the feeling of dependence lies at the root of all religious worship, and that however high the spiritual life might rise it must always begin with a deep sense of a great need which only God could satisfy. If this sense of need and a feeling of dependence are at the root of natural religion it is not hard to see why the great god Entertainment is so ardently worshiped by so many. For there are millions who cannot live without amusement; life without some form of entertainment for them is simply intolerable; they look forward to the blessed relief afforded by professional entertainers and other forms of psychological narcotics as a dope addict looks to his daily shot of heroin. Without them they could not summon courage to face existence. (*The Root of the Righteous*, p. 31)

Entertainment Is a Symptom

This is the cause of a very serious breakdown in modern evangelicalism. The idea of cultivation and exercise, so dear to the saints of old, has now no place in our total religious picture. It is too slow, too common. We now demand glamour and fast flowing dramatic action. A generation of Christians reared among push buttons and automatic machines is impatient of slower and less direct methods of reaching their goals. We have been trying to apply machine-age methods to our relations with God. We read our chapter, have our short devotions and rush away, hoping to make up for our deep inward bankruptcy by attending another gospel meeting or listening to another thrilling story told by a religious adventurer lately returned from afar.

The tragic results of this spirit are all about us: shallow loves, hollow religious philosophies, the preponderance of the element of fun in gospel meetings, the glorification of men, trust in religious externalities, quasi-religious fellowships, salesmanship methods, the mistaking of dynamic personality for the power of the Spirit. These and such as these are the symptoms of an evil disease, a deep and serious malady of the soul. (*The Pursuit of God*, pp. 62-63)

The Danger of Overreacting

We have already seen the reaction [the denial of spiritual longing and desire] among the masses of evangelical Christians. There has been a revolt in two directions, a rather unconscious revolt, like the gasping of fish in a bowl where there is no oxygen. A great company of evangelicals have already gone over into the area of religious entertainment so that many gospel churches are tramping on the doorstep of the theater. Over against that, some serious segments of fundamental and evangelical thought have revolted into the position of evangelical rationalism which finds it a practical thing to make peace with liberalism. (*The Tozer Pulpit*, Book 4, p. 88)

Pressure on Religious Leaders

Pastors and churches in our hectic times are harassed by the temptation to seek size at any cost and to secure by inflation what they cannot gain by legitimate growth. The mixed multitude cries for quantity and will not forgive a minister who insists upon solid values and permanence. Many a man of God is being subjected to cruel pressure by the ill-taught members of his flock who scorn his slow methods and demand quick results and a popular following regardless of quality. These children play in the marketplaces and cannot overlook the affront we do them by our refusal to dance when they whistle or to weep when they out of caprice pipe a sad tune. They are greedy for thrills, and since they dare no longer seek them in the theater, they demand to have them brought into the church. (*The Next Chapter after the Last*, p. 8)

Does Not Belong in Church

A church fed on excitement is no New Testament church at all. The desire for surface stimulation is a sure mark of the fallen nature, the very thing Christ died to deliver us from. A curious crowd of baptized worldlings waiting each Sunday for the quasi-religious needle to give them a lift bears no relation whatsoever to a true assembly of Christian believers. And that its members protest their undying faith in the Bible does not change things any. "Not everyone that saith unto me, Lord, Lord, shall enter into the kingdom of heaven but he that doeth the will of my Father which is in heaven." (*The Next Chapter after the Last*, p. 14)

Pray for Conviction

Let's pray that God will bring conviction on the world. Let's pray that He will send conviction back. Religion has become so popular now that it is shown in theaters, sung over radio and in barn dances. Just one more form of entertainment. We fundamentals and evangelicals just will not believe the truth about ourselves and the kind of people we are. So we have a popular religion but very little power because we have very little conviction, very little repentance and very little sorrow. (Sermon, "Men Do Not Believe the Truth about Themselves," John 8:38, General Council)

The old writers talked about the dark night of the soul. A time of emptying. A time when it became dark all around us. But we're too carnal to allow our hearts to get dark longing for God now. We're so determined we want to be happy that if we can't be happy by the Holy Ghost we'll drum up our happiness. Religious "Rock and Rollers"! We're going to get happy somehow if we've got to beat it up with a tom-tom. You can have that kind of happiness if you want it, but if you don't want it and are dissatisfied with it and you want the joy that comes out of Joseph's new tomb open now forever, if you want the joy that comes from the Holy Ghost, a well of water springing up within you forever, then you will likely have a loneliness and an inner darkness and a despair with self and you'll wonder what happened to you and you'll say, "Am I backsliding?" No, you're not backsliding. You are going on with God. ("The Holy Spirit," Sermon #6, Romans 12:1-2, Toronto)

Don't Seek Entertainment

There is a cross for you and me and there is a cross for every one of us. And that cross is subjective and internal and experiential. . . . That cross is that which we voluntarily take up—that's hard and bitter and distasteful—that we do for Christ's sake and suffer the consequences and despise the shame. . . .

But the evangelicals of which we are a part say, "Let the cross kill Jesus but we will live on and be happy and have fun." But the cross on the hill has got to become the cross in the heart. When the cross on the hill has been transformed by the miraculous grace of the Holy Ghost into the cross in the heart, then we begin to know something of what it means and it will become to us the cross of power. (Sermon #40 on Hebrews, Toronto)

We have the breezy, self-confident Christians with little affinity for Christ and His cross. We have the joy-bell boys that can bounce out there and look as much like a game show host as possible. Yet, they are doing it for Jesus' sake?! The hypocrites! They're not doing it for Jesus' sake at all; they are doing it in their own carnal flesh and are using the church as a theater because they haven't yet reached the place where the legitimate theater would take them. (Sermon, "Complete Surrender," Chicago)

Religious shows leave a bad flavor. When they enter the holy place, they come perilously near to offering strange fire to the Lord. At their worst they are sacrilege; always they are unnecessary, and at their best they are a poor substitute for prayer and the Holy Ghost. Church plays are invariably cheap and amateurish, and in addition to grieving the Holy Ghost, those who attend them are cheated by getting wretchedly poor entertainment for their money. (*The Early Tozer: A Word in Season*, p. 98)

Not Real Joy

The reason evangelical Christianity has so many cowbells and handsaws and shows and films and funny gadgets and celebrated men and women to stir them up is because they don't have the joy of the Lord. A happy man doesn't need very much else. (Sermon, "Fruit of the Spirit," Chicago)

We don't have joy so we try to create it, and I think that God in His heaven is probably more kind and patient about all this than I am. But I think that even God must get awfully sick of what He sees: all the little cowbells we have to jingle to try to be happy when we are simply missing the fountain of happiness that ought to spring from within. When the well of joy isn't flowing, we try to paint the pump in order to get a little joy or tack jingle bells on the old pump handle, but it doesn't bring the water up. (Sermon, "Fruit of the Spirit," Chicago)

[Christianity has seen] a steady decline in the quality of Christian worship on the one hand and, on the other, the rise of religious entertainment as a source of mental pleasure. Wise leaders should have known that the human heart cannot exist in a vacuum. If men do not have joy in their hearts they will seek it somewhere else. If Christians are forbidden to enjoy the wine of the Spirit they will turn to the wine of the flesh for enjoyment. And that is exactly what fundamental Christianity (as well as the so-called "full gospel" groups) has done in the last quarter century. God's people have turned to the amusements of the world to try to squeeze a bit of juice out of them for the relief of their dry and joyless hearts. "Gospel" boogie singing now furnishes for many persons the only religious joy they know. Others wipe their eyes tenderly over "gospel" movies, and a countless number of amusements flourish everywhere, paid for by the consecrated tithes of persons who ought to know better. Our teachers took away our right to be happy in God, and the human heart wreaked its terrible vengeance by going on a fleshly binge from which the evangelical Church will not soon recover, if indeed it ever does. For multitudes of professed Christians today the Holy Spirit is not a necessity. They have learned to cheer their hearts and warm their hands at other fires. And scores of publishers and various grades

of "producers" are waxing fat on their delinquency. (*The Root of the Righteous*, p. 69)

Tozer Attacks Amateurism

The church today is suffering from a rash of
amateurism. Any untrained, unprepared, unspiritual, empty rattletrap of a fellow who is a bit ambitious can start himself something religious.
Then we all listen to him, pay him for it, promote
him and work to try to help this fellow who never
heard from God in the first place. Amateurism
has gone mad, gone wild. That's because we are
not worshipers. Nobody who worships God is
likely to do anything off beat or out of place. Nobody who is a true worshiper indeed is likely to
give himself up to carnal and worldly religious
projects. ("The Chief End of Man," Sermon #4,
Toronto, 1962)

Because we are not worshipers we are wasting
other people's money tremendously. We're mark-
ing time, we're spinning our wheels with the axles
up on blocks, burning the gasoline and making a
noise and getting no place. God calls us to worship and I find this missing in the Church of the
Lord Jesus Christ in this day. Instead of worship,
we are now second in entertainment to the theaters. I want to tell you something. If I want to see
a show I know where I can see a good one put on
by top flight geniuses who know what they are
doing. If I want a show I'll duck out and go down
to a theater and see a show hot out of Hollywood

or London by men and women who are artists in their field. I will not go to a church and see a lot of ham actors putting on a home talent show. And yet, that's where we are in evangelical circles. We've got more show in evangelical circles than anywhere else. ("The Chief End of Man," Sermon #4, Toronto, 1962)

When I say we are suffering from a rash of amateurism, I mean that we like to have just everybody, anything, anyway worship. It can't be. You must prepare yourself to worship God. That preparation is not always a pleasant thing. There must be some revolutionary changes in your life. There must be some things destroyed in your life. ("The Chief End of Man," Sermon #6, Toronto, 1962)

We are not a religious theater to provide a place for amateur entertainers to display their talents. ("The Chief End of Man," Sermon #10, Toronto, 1962)

Worship Is Not Entertainment

I hope that we will remove from our hearts every ugly thing and every unbeautiful thing and every dead thing and every unholy thing that might prevent us from worshiping the Lord Jesus Christ in the beauty of holiness. Now I am quite sure that this kind of thing is not popular. The world does not want to hear it and the half-saved churches of the evangelical fold do not want to hear it. They want to be entertained while they are edified. Entertain me and edify me without pain. ("The Chief End of Man," Sermon #9, Toronto, 1962)

A crass example of the modern effort to use God for selfish purposes is the well-known comedian who, after repeated failures, promised someone he called God that if He would help him to make good in the entertainment world he would repay Him by giving generously to the care of sick children. Shortly afterward he hit the big time in the night clubs and on television. He has kept his word and is raising large sums of money to build children's hospitals. These contributions to charity, he feels, are a small price to pay for a success in one of the sleaziest fields of human endeavor.

One might excuse the act of this entertainer as something to be expected of a twentieth-century pagan; but that multitudes of evangelicals in North America should actually believe that God had something to do with the whole business is not so easily overlooked. This low and false view of Deity is one major reason for the immense popularity God enjoys these days among well-fed Westerners. (*Man: The Dwelling Place of God*, pp. 57-58)

The average Christian is like a kitten that has found a ball of yarn and has played with the yarn and romped until it is wrapped in a cocoon. The kitten cannot get itself out. It just lies there and whimpers. Somebody has to come unwind it. We have tried to be simple, but instead of being simple we have simplified—we have not become simple. We are sophisticated and overly complex.

We have simplified until Christianity amounts to this: God is love; Jesus died for you; believe, accept, be jolly, have fun and tell others. And away we go—that is the Christianity of our day. I would not give a plug nickel for the whole business of it. Once in a while God has a poor bleeding sheep that manages to live on that kind of thing and we wonder how. (*Rut, Rot or Revival*, p. 173)

Because we are not truly worshipers, we spend a lot of time in the churches just spinning our wheels, burning the gasoline, making a noise but not getting anywhere.

Oh, brother or sister, God calls us to worship, but in many instances we are in entertainment, just running a poor second to the theaters.

That is where we are, even in the evangelical churches, and I don't mind telling you that most of the people we say we are trying to reach will never come to a church to see a lot of amateur actors putting on a home-talent show. (*Whatever Happened to Worship?*, p. 17)

So many churches and other religious structures are being built these days that the building industry, which once considered such things something of a dead weight, is pretty well steamed up about the whole thing and is now quite eager to have the religious trade. Church membership is growing out of all proportion to the growth of the population. Converts to one or another religion are being sought on every level of society and among all classes and age groups. We have zealous work going on among children and young people. We are using sound trucks, radio, television, streetcar cards, billboards, neon signs, messages in bottles and on balloons. We are using trained horses, trained dogs, trained canaries, ventriloquists, magicians and drama to stir up religious interest. Innumerable professional guilds, industrial clubs and businessmen's and women's committees have sprung up to provide spiritual fellowship for religious-minded persons engaged in the various pursuits of life. Religious songs are in the repertoire of many professional entertainers. Religion is being plugged by nightclub entertainers, prize-fighters, movie stars and by at least one incarcerated gangster who has up to this time shown no sorrow for his way of life and no evidence of repentance. Religion, if you please, is now big business. (*The Price of Neglect*, p. 83)

Entertainment in the Church

For centuries the Church stood solidly against every form of worldly entertainment, recognizing it for what it was—a device for wasting time, a refuge from the disturbing voice of conscience, a scheme to divert attention from moral accountability. For this she got herself abused roundly by the sons of this world. But of late she has become tired of the abuse and has given over the struggle. She appears to have decided that if she cannot conquer the great god Entertainment she may as well join forces with him and make whatever use she can of his powers. So today we have the astonishing spectacle of millions of dollars being poured into the unholy job of providing earthly entertainment for the so-called sons of heaven. Religious entertainment is in many places rapidly crowding out the serious things of God. Many churches these days have become little more than poor theaters where fifth-rate "producers" peddle their shoddy wares with the full approval of evangelical leaders who can even quote a holy text in defense of their delinquency. And hardly a man dares raise his voice against it. (*The Root of the Righteous*, p. 32)

The great god Entertainment amuses his devotees mainly by telling them stories. The love of stories, which is characteristic of childhood, has taken fast hold of the minds of the retarded saints of our day, so much so that not a few persons manage to make a comfortable living by spinning yarns and serving them up in various disguises to church people. What is natural and beautiful in a child may be shocking when it persists into adulthood, and more so when it appears in the sanctuary and seeks to pass for true religion. (*The Root of the Righteous*, p. 33)

The cross stands high above the opinions of men and to that cross all opinions must come at last for judgment. A shallow and worldly leadership would modify the cross to please the entertainment-mad saintlings who will have their fun even within the very sanctuary; but to do so is to court spiritual disaster and risk the anger of the Lamb turned Lion. (*The Root of the Righteous*, p. 63)

It is because there are so many of these ignoble saintlets, these miniature editions of the Christian way, demanding that Christianity must be fun, that distinct organizations have been launched to give it to them. Yes, there are organizations that exist for the sole purpose of mixing religion and fun for our Christian young people. (*The Tozer Pulpit*, Book 8, p. 28)

Christianity to the average evangelical church member is simply an avenue to a good and pleasant time, with a little biblical devotional material thrown in for good measure! (*The Tozer Pulpit*, Book 6, p. 72)

I cannot determine when I will die. But I hope I do not live to see the day when God has to turn from men and women who have heard His holy truth and have played with it, fooled with it and equated it with fun and entertainment and religious nonsense.

We cannot deny that this attitude is found in much of current Christianity. As a result, people have hardened their hearts to the point that they no longer hear the voice of God. (*Jesus Is Victor*, p. 130)

The church is not simply a religious institution. It is not a religious theater where performers are paid to amuse those who attend. It is an assembly of redeemed sinners—men and women called unto Christ and commissioned to spread His gospel to the ends of the earth. (*Jesus Is Victor*, p. 152)

Heresy in the Church

Religious entertainment has so corrupted the Church of Christ that millions don't know that it's a heresy. Millions of evangelicals throughout the world have devoted themselves to religious entertainment. They don't know that it's as much heresy as the counting of beads or the splashing of holy water or something else. To expose this, of course, raises a storm of angry protest among the people. (*Success and the Christian*, p. 6)

One man wrote an article as an exposé of me. He said that I claimed that religious entertainment was wrong and he said, "Don't you know that every time you sing a hymn, it's entertainment?" Every time you sing a hymn? I don't know how that fellow ever finds his way home at night. He ought to have a seeing eye dog and a man with a white cane to take him home!

When you raise your eyes to God and sing, "Break thou the bread of life, dear Lord, to me," is that entertainment—or is it worship? Isn't there a difference between worship and entertainment? The church that can't worship must be entertained. And men who can't lead a church to worship must provide the entertainment. That is why we have the great evangelical heresy here today—the heresy of religious entertainment. (*Success and the Christian*, pp. 6-7)

If a gospel troupe comes along, you're satisfied for a while, because they have cowbells and a musical handsaw and a lot of other gadgets.

Actually, you can catch them at the Eighth Street theater any night by just writing in for tickets. I can't think of a single one of their names, but I know they are down there with the cowbells and banjos and their hillbilly songs, and if that's what you want, go down there and get it.

But I say that if the gospel proclamation has to bring that in in order to get a crowd, boycott it. (*The Tozer Pulpit*, Book 1, p. 139)

Worldly Programs

Evangelical Christianity is gasping for breath for we happen to have come upon us a period when it is a popular thing to sing about tears and prayers and believing. You can get a religious phrase kicked around almost anywhere right in the middle of a worldly program dedicated to the world, the flesh and the devil. Old Mammon with two silver dollars for eyes sits at the top of it, lying about the quality of the products, shamelessly praising actors who ought to be put to work laying bricks. In the middle of it, someone will say with an unctuous voice, trained in a studio to sound religious, "Now, our hymn for the week!" So they break in, and the band goes, "Twinkle, twankle, twinkle, twankle"—and they sing something that the devil must blush to hear. They call that religion, and I will admit that, all right, but it isn't salvation and it isn't Christianity and it isn't the Holy Ghost. It isn't New Testament and it isn't redemption—it is simply making capital out of religion for a price. (*The Tozer Pulpit*, Book 3, p. 34)

Why should believing Christians want everything pre-cooked, pre-digested, sliced and salted, and expect that God must come and help us eat and hold the food to our baby lips while we pound the table and splash—and we think that is Christianity! Brethren, it is not. It is a degenerate bastard breed that has no right to be called Christianity. (*The Tozer Pulpit*, Book 3, p. 37)

Anyone who needs to be chucked under the chin all the time to keep him happy and satisfied is in bad shape spiritually. He can ignore the fact that the Bible urges us to go on unto perfection for he is of that part of the church that cannot be satisfied without a visit from the latest gospel peddler, who promises cowbells, a musical handsaw and a lot of other novelties! (*The Tozer Pulpit*, Book 5, pp. 42-43)

Sinful Pleasures

Religious fiction . . . makes use of sex to interest the reading public, the paper-thin excuse being that if romance and religion are woven into a story the average person who would not read a purely religious book will read the story and thus be exposed to the gospel. Leaving aside the fact that most modern religious novelists are home talent amateurs, scarcely one of whom is capable of writing a single line of even fair literature, the whole concept behind the religio-romantic novel is unsound. The libidinous impulses and the sweet, deep movings of the Holy Spirit are diametrically opposed to each other. The notion that Eros can be made to serve as an assistant of the Lord of glory is outrageous. The "Christian" film that seeks to draw customers by picturing amorous love scenes in its advertising is completely false to the religion of Christ. Only the spiritually blind will be taken in by it. (*Born after Midnight*, p. 38)

One of the very greatest calamities which sin has brought upon us is the debasement of our normal emotions. We laugh at things which are not funny; we find pleasure in acts which are beneath our human dignity; and we rejoice in objects which should have no place in our affections. The objection to "sinful pleasures" which has been characteristic of the true saint, is at bottom simply a protest against the degradation of our human emotions. That gambling, for instance, should be allowed to engross the interests of men made in the image of God has seemed like a horrible perversion of noble powers; that alcohol should be necessary to stimulate the feeling of pleasure has seemed like a kind of prostitution; that men should turn to the man-made theater for enjoyment has seemed an affront to the God who placed us in the midst of a universe charged with high dramatic action. The world's artificial pleasures are all but evidence that the human race has to a large extent lost its power to enjoy the true pleasures of life and is forced to substitute for them false and degrading thrills. (*God's Pursuit of Man*, pp. 107-108)

Human Talent or Spiritual Gifts?

We hear that some fellow can whistle through his teeth. Someone else has marvelous talent for impromptu composition of poetry. Some musicians are talented players and singers. Others are talented talkers (Let us admit it!). So in this realm of religious activity, talent runs the church. The gifts of the Spirit are not recognized and used as God intended. . . .

A Christian congregation can survive and often appear to prosper in the community by the exercise of human talent and without any touch from the Holy Spirit. But it is simply religious activity, and the dear people will not know anything better until the great and terrible day when our self-employed talents are burned with fire and only what was wrought by the Holy Spirit will stand. (*Tragedy in the Church: The Missing Gifts*, p. 23)

Extra-scriptural Claptrap

This church ought to be a place that is lighted by the light of the world shed forth by the Holy Spirit. It is where we gather at intervals to eat of the bread of life, not only on communion Sunday, but all the time, every Sunday. It ought to be where the altar of incense sends up its sweet spirals of fragrant perfume sweet to God and pleasant in His nostrils, and the sound of prayer pleasant in His ear and the sight of enlightened people gathered together pleasant to His eyes.

This is the only kind of church that I'm interested in. I'm not interested when you have to go out and bring somebody in from the outside and say, "Will you come and perform for us?" Can you imagine a priest bringing a clown and saying to the clown, "Now come, clown into the holy place. Be reverent and do it for Jesus' sake." And when that clown came in there was light, the light that lighted every man, light that never was on land or sea. "And here is the bread. Reverently we may eat and live forever. Here is the altar of incense where we can send up our prayers to the ears of God, and now the clown will do his part."

I would walk five miles to keep from seeing him or hearing him and I wouldn't walk one inch to see him and I wouldn't give one dime to support him. All of this extra-scriptural claptrap that has been dragged into the church in recent times grieves the Holy Ghost. We have muted the lights, the bread has gotten stale and the altar of incense has lost its fragrance. (Sermon #24 on Hebrews, Toronto)

Those Christians who belong to the evangelical wing of the Church (which I firmly believe is the only one that even approximates New Testament Christianity) have over the last half-century shown an increasing impatience with things invisible and eternal and have demanded and got a host of things visible and temporal to satisfy their fleshly appetites. Without biblical authority, or any other right under the sun, carnal religious leaders have introduced a host of attractions that serve no purpose except to provide entertainment for the retarded saints.

It is now common practice in most evangelical churches to offer the people, especially the young people, a maximum of entertainment and a minimum of serious instruction. It is scarcely possible in most places to get anyone to attend a meeting where the only attraction is God. One can only conclude that God's professed children are bored with Him, for they must be wooed to meeting with a stick of striped candy in the form of religious movies, games and refreshments.

This has influenced the whole pattern of church life, and even brought into being a new type of church architecture, designed to house the golden calf.

So we have the strange anomaly of orthodoxy in

creed and heterodoxy in practice. The striped-candy technique has been so fully integrated into our present religious thinking that it is simply taken for granted. Its victims never dream that it is not a part of the teachings of Christ and His apostles.

Any objection to the carryings on of our present gold-calf Christianity is met with the triumphant reply, "But we are winning them!" And winning them to what? To true discipleship? To cross-carrying? To self-denial? To separation from the world? To crucifixion of the flesh? To holy living? To nobility of character? To a despising of the world's treasures? To hard self-discipline? To love for God? To total committal to Christ? Of course the answer to all these questions is no. (*Man: The Dwelling Place of God*, p. 136)

Programs Replace Worship

Thanks to our splendid Bible societies and to other effective agencies for dissemination of the Word, there are today many millions of people who hold "right opinions," probably more than ever before in the history of the Church. Yet I wonder if there was ever a time when true spiritual worship was at a lower ebb. To great sections of the Church the art of worship has been lost entirely, and in its place has come that strange and foreign thing called the "program." This word has been borrowed from the stage and applied with sad wisdom to the type of public service which now passes for worship among us. (*The Pursuit of God*, p. 9)

Chapter 12

Propaganda, Popular Religion and Programs

Beware of Propaganda

The world is using the Church in our day to achieve its ends. Here was the scarlet woman [in Revelation] and the world used her. They exalted her to sit on many waters and they used her to achieve their ends and then when they had done what they wanted to do, they turned on her and they hated her and made her desolate and naked and they burned her with fire. As long as religious people can be the pawns and catpaws of the propagandists and can be made useful they will be put up with. But if ever we cross them in anything or oppose them or dare to stand up as free men in God and say, "That isn't the way I see it," we'll be branded as another sect and despised and given the silent treatment. The press gives space to those they can use and the silent treatment to those they cannot. (Sermon, "Resisting the World's Propaganda," General Council)

The devil is busy brainwashing us and conditioning us little by little and feeding his ideas into the Church. The counsel of the ungodly comes and as the ideas of the ungodly enter the Church the ideas of God go out. As the counsel of the ungodly come in, the counsel of God goes out. My crusade in the day in which I live is to wake the Church and rouse it to the fact that it is being brainwashed and propagandized into accepting that which it would never accept if it were a law in Washington. (Sermon, "Resisting the World's Propaganda," General Council)

Needed: Humble Leaders

In this day when shimmering personalities carry on the Lord's work after the methods of the entertainment world, it is refreshing to associate for a moment even in the pages of a book with a sincere and humble man who keeps his own personality out of sight and places the emphasis upon the inworking of God. It is our belief that the evangelical movement will continue to drift farther and farther from the New Testament position unless its leadership passes from the modern religious star to the self-effacing saint who asks for no praise and seeks no place, happy only when the glory is attributed to God and himself forgotten. (*Of God and Men*, p. 18)

Don't Aim to Be Socially Acceptable

Our pitiful effort to make Christianity socially acceptable is an effort worse than wasted. To make out of the cross a symbol and relegate its nails and thorns and blood and terror and ostracism back to the hill above Jerusalem and forget that that same cross is alive today wherever the gospel is preached is to commit a deadly theological error. And yet it's what we hear most of the time.

They don't crucify people now because they can get along with them too easily. There is too much collaboration between men who claim to follow the Crucified One and the people who don't believe in the Crucified One. Wherever they can catch a Christlike man they run for the nails and hammer. What we need (and I don't have the courage to pray for it) in our day is to have more Christians crucified. We need more persecution. We need a social situation that makes it dangerous to be a Christian. It isn't dangerous now; it's quite the popular thing.

They use a preacher now for almost anything. They can't cut a tape without having a preacher there to cut the tape. They can't break ground for anything—the latest dog pound—but what the reverend has to be there to say a prayer and break the first steamshovel full while he looks up and smirks at the camera. Ladies can't begin their campaign to drive all the ground moles out of Cook County except to have a pastor there to mumble a few words, smile and look religious.

But nobody crucifies the "old boy," they get along with him. (Sermon, "Voices That Entreat Us: The Holy Spirit," Chicago, 1953)

Popular Christianity parrots the language of New Testament theology, but it accepts the world's opinion of itself and sedulously apes its ways (except for a few evil practices which even the world itself admits are wrong). Then Christ is offered as something added, a Friend up there, a Guarantor against the time when the tumult and the shouting dies and we are called in from the playground and forced to go to sleep. (*God Tells the Man Who Cares*, p. 17)

Never imagine that the cross of Christ will become socially acceptable. That which is of Adam will always persecute that which is of Christ. He that is born once will always persecute him who is born twice. (Sermon, "The Man Who Exalted God," Wheaton College, 1961)

Publicity Is Worshiped

Publicity is worshiped like a god. To be known in the gates, to get your picture in the papers, to have somebody quote you, to imagine you are somebody—that's publicity. It's worshiped like a god and success is courted like a street walker. . . . The secret dream of our young people is not to be saintly but to get into pictures. And the only reason they don't is because they can't. (Sermon, "He Must Increase," Chicago, 1956)

The modern effort to popularize the Christian faith has been extremely damaging to that faith. The purpose has been to simplify truth for the masses by using the language of the masses instead of the language of the church. It has not succeeded, but has added to rather than diminished religious confusion. (*The Set of the Sail*, p. 159)

Jesus Betrayed for Popularity

People today are betraying Jesus who have nothing against Jesus, who will even speak kindly about Jesus. There are people singing about Jesus on the radio now who have walked out of church choirs. Leading sopranos or tenors or altos or basses have walked out of church choirs and sold themselves to the beer interest and are singing anthems now that sell beer to the public. They've nothing against Jesus and in a tender moment they sing and speak kindly of Jesus. Their reason for betraying Him is not that they hated Him but that they wanted money. There are people who betrayed Jesus because they wanted to be popular with their high school crowd. They've nothing against Him and if anybody said anything against Jesus they would fight for Him; they would stand up and say, "Now I'm not a Christian but I know better than that." They would defend Jesus if it ever came to that. They have a kind feeling toward Him, but they want to be popular with their crowd. They want to stand well with the kids. They want to stand well with the business people with whom they work or the office where they work or the little group in their social circles. So they betray Jesus for popularity and to keep friends and to keep from many enemies. (Sermon, "The Great Double Cross," Chicago, 1956)

Dictatorship of Programs

Every age has its own characteristics. Right now we are in an age of religious complexity. The simplicity which is in Christ is rarely found among us. In its stead are programs, methods, organizations and a world of nervous activities which occupy time and attention but can never satisfy the longing of the heart. The shallowness of our inner experience, the hallowness of our worship and that servile imitation of the world which marks our promotional methods all testify that we, in this day, know God only imperfectly, and the peace of God scarcely at all. (*The Pursuit of God*, p. 17)

The treacherous enemy facing the church of Jesus Christ today is the dictatorship of the routine, when the routine becomes "lord" in the life of the church. Programs are organized and the prevailing conditions are accepted as normal. Anyone can predict next Sunday's service and what will happen. This seems to be the most deadly threat in the church today. When we come to the place where everything can be predicted and nobody expects anything unusual from God, we are in a rut. The routine dictates, and we can tell not only what will happen next Sunday, but will occur

next month and, if things do not improve, what
will take place next year. Then we have reached
the place where what has been determines what
is, and what is determines what will be. (*Rut, Rot
or Revival*, p. 6)

In our churches we have fairly well pro-
grammed ourselves into deadness and apathy.
Think of this little woman [at the well] running to
testify with the good news brimming over in her
soul. If someone had halted her by taking hold of
her garment as she ran, and said: "Sister, we are
glad to see the new light in your face, and we
would like to have you third on the program," she
would have died along with those scribes and Sa-
maritans and all the rest. (*The Tozer Pulpit*, Book 3,
pp. 111-112)

Chapter 13

An Outward Shift

Too Much Comfort

Another reason for the absence of real yearning for Christ's return is that Christians are so comfortable in this world that they have little desire to leave it. For those leaders who set the pace of religion and determine its content and quality, Christianity has become of late remarkably lucrative. The streets of gold do not have too great an appeal for those who find it so easy to pile up gold and silver in the service of the Lord here on earth. We all want to reserve the hope of heaven as a kind of insurance against the day of death but as long as we are healthy and comfortable, why change a familiar good for something about which we actually know very little? So reasons the carnal mind, and so subtly that we are scarcely aware of it.

Again, in these times religion has become jolly good fun right here in this present world, and what's the hurry about heaven anyway? Christianity, contrary to what some had thought, is another and higher form of entertainment. Christ has done all the suffering. He has shed all the tears and carried all the crosses; we have but to enjoy the benefits of His heartbreak in the form of religious pleasures modeled after the world but carried on in the name of Jesus. So say the same people who claim to believe in Christ's second coming. (*Born after Midnight*, p. 134)

External Appeals

Our trouble is that we are trying to confirm the truth of Christianity by an appeal to external evidence. We are saying, "Well, look at this fellow. He can throw a baseball farther than anybody else and he is a Christian, therefore Christianity must be true." "Here is a great statesman who believes the Bible. Therefore the Bible must be true." We quote Daniel Webster or Roger Bacon. We write books to show that some scientist believed in Christianity: Therefore Christianity must be true. We are all the way out on the wrong track, brother! That is not New Testament Christianity at all. That is a pitiful, whimpering, drooling appeal to the flesh. That never was the testimony of the New Testament, never the way God did things—never! You might satisfy the intellects of men by external evidences, and Christ did, I say, point to external evidence when He was here on earth. But He said, "I am sending you something better. I am taking Christian apologetics out of the realm of logic and putting it into the realm of life. I am proving My deity, and My proof will not be an appeal to a general or a prime minister. The proof lies in an invisible, unseen but powerful energy that visits the human soul when the gospel is preached—the Holy Ghost!" The Spirit of the living God brought an evidence that needed no logic; it went straight to the soul like a flash of silver light, like the direct plunge of a sharp spear into the heart. Those are the very words that the Scriptures use when it says "pierced (pricked) to the heart." One translator points out that that word "pricked" is a word that means that it goes in deeper than the spear that pierced Jesus' side. (*How to Be Filled with the Holy Spirit*, pp. 29-31)

An Outward Shift

All of this top-heavy Christendom that we know today was never known in the book of Acts and in the days of the apostles. Utter simplicity was at the root of everything. Faith was the power, or at least the instrument, and the Holy Ghost the power that led them on and love throbbed at the heart of their worship and purity of life was demanded of them. So they had worship and love and faith and their moral lives were pure and their whole lives simple. And then as the years passed came the shift in externalism just as had happened in the days of Israel. A shift outward from the center toward the surface. Always remember this, that it could be the easiest thing in the world to live at the center but it usually is the hardest. It's easier to live on the surface than it is in the center. The Church shifted toward externalism and institutionalism took over. Then came form and ceremony and tradition. (Sermon, "The Deeper Life," Chicago, 1956)

Then came a slow shift from the center out toward the perimeter. Out from the beating heart, out to the epidermis, to the outside skin of things. Then externalism took over in Israel and a good deal of the long history of Israel in the Old Testament is the history of Israel yielding to the propensity to live on the surface and the prophets of God urging Israel back to the center. Always God urges men back to the center and always men by centrifugal force tend to fly out to the edge of things. Always God wants men to have content and always men seek to be satisfied with words. (Sermon, "The Deeper Life," Chicago, 1956)

The whole problem is the externality of worship. This is the biggest problem the church faces now—the problem of externalism. ("The Chief End of Man," Sermon #7, Toronto, 1962)

Form without Worship

Men like ceremony without love or meaning and God always insists on love and meaning regardless of ceremony. And men love form without worship and God wants worship whether He has form or not. And externalism lies in words and ceremonies and forms. Internalism lies in content, in love, in worship, in inward spiritual reality. (Sermon, "The Deeper Life," Chicago, 1956)

Dry Worship without the Spirit

Then, also, the Spirit gave a bright, emotional quality to their religion, and I grieve before my God over the lack of this in our day. The emotional quality isn't there. There is a sickliness about us all; we pump so hard trying to get a little drop of delight out of our old rusty well, and we write innumerable bouncy choruses, and we pump and pump until you can hear the old rusty thing squeak across forty acres. But it doesn't work. (*How to Be Filled with the Holy Spirit*, p. 14)

I have noticed lately among so-called evangelicals a renewed interest in the religious gadgets that our Protestant fathers once threw away to make room for the Holy Spirit. It is becoming more common now to see in our churches huge pictures of Christ, crosses on the altar, candles and other symbolic objects. This is the sure way back to formalism and death. In proportion as the presence of Christ is felt in a congregation these things will be unnecessary, even offensive. And as the Presence lifts and withdraws, these symbols are brought in as poor substitutes. (*The Size of the Soul*, p. 169)

People have made a comedy of religion. A comedy of errors it has been, too, because men have enslaved themselves to externals. They have enslaved themselves to objects. ("The Chief End of Man," Sermon #7, Chicago, 1956)

Swimming against the Current

The fish that goes along with the current hasn't any trouble with the current, but as soon as he starts the other way the current gets sore at him. Just as long as you go the way the wind blows, everybody will say you're very fine and commend you for being deeply religious. If you decide to go God's way instead of the way the wind blows they'll say that your roof leaks or that something has happened to you that you're a fanatic. You can go along with the times or you can be like Zechariah and Elizabeth and refuse to go along with the times. Personally I've decided that a long time ago. They say that if you don't conform to the times and find a common ground for getting along with everybody that nobody will listen to you. The more I'm nonconformist the more people want to hear me. (Sermon, "To Older People," Mahaffey Camp)

I've been told that I've missed the boat but I reply that I wasn't trying to catch that boat. That boat and a lot of others like it can go on without me and I'll be quite happy. We can conform to the religion of our times if we want to.

I weigh 145 pounds dripping wet, but I stand here to tell you that I'm a nonconformist, twice born, and a rebel and I will not conform to the times. Up to now I've been able to get a hearing and refused to conform to the times. But if a day ever comes when to conform to the times is the price you have to pay to be heard, then I'll go out and start where I started before on the street corner and preach there. But I won't conform to the times.

They say you are supposed to do it. They say, "Don't you know we have the same message but it's just different times we're living in." I know the voice of the serpent when I hear it. The hiss of the serpent is in that and I recognize that. So we can either conform or we can withdraw from the whole business, and Paul says, "From such turn away." (Sermon, "To Older People," Mahaffey Camp)

We cannot afford to let down our Christian standards just to hold the interest of people who want to go to hell and still belong to a church. We have had carnal and fleshly and self-loving people who wanted to come in and control young people's groups and liberate us from our spiritual life and standards and "strictness." (*The Tozer Pulpit*, Book 6, p. 32)

Too Much Soft Preaching

In our day, the churches are trying to offer such a blend and such a compromise between heaven and hell. Some pastors feel that this is the way to get along with people and to improve the church's public relations. (*The Tozer Pulpit, Book 3*, p. 91)

By offering our hearers a sweetness-and-light

gospel and promising every taker a place on the sunny side of the brae, we not only cruelly deceive them, we guarantee also a high casualty rate among the converts won on such terms. On certain foreign fields the expression "rice Christians" has been coined to describe those who adopt Christianity for profit. The experienced missionary knows that the convert that must pay a heavy price for his faith in Christ is the one who will persevere to the end. He begins with the wind in his face, and should the storm grow in strength he will not turn back for he has been conditioned to endure it. (*That Incredible Christian*, p. 116)

Don't Compromise

The rise of a new religious spirit in recent years is marked by disturbing similarities to that earlier "revival" under Constantine. Now as then a quasi-Christianity is achieving acceptance by compromise. It is dickering with the unregenerate world for acceptance and, as someone said recently, it is offering Christ at bargain prices to win customers. The total result is a conglomerate religious mess that cannot but make the reverent Christian sick in his heart. (*The Price of Neglect*, p. 95)

We are sent to bless the world, but never are we told to compromise with it. Our glory lies in a spiritual withdrawal from all that builds on dust. The bee finds no honey while crawling around the hive. Honey is in the flower far away where there is quiet and peace and the sun and the flowing stream; there the bee must go to find it. The Christian will find slim pickings where professed believers play and pray all in one breath. He may be compelled sometimes to travel alone or at least to go with the ostracized few. To belong to the despised minority may be the price he must pay for power. But power is cheap at any price. (*The Next Chapter after the Last*, p. 21)

Chapter 14

Modern Evangelism

Preach the Whole Message

Neo-Christianity, which seems for the time to be the most popular (and is certainly the most aggressive), is very careful not to oppose sin. It wins its crowds by amusing them and its converts by hiding from them the full implications of the Christian message. It carries on its projects after the ballyhoo methods of American business. (*The Next Chapter after the Last*, p. 18)

The feeling that we've got to make converts at any cost has greatly wounded the Church of Christ. We must present the truth as we are told to present it and let the Holy Ghost work and the individual man decide whether he will accept it or not. This soft, pussy idea that in order to keep people coming and giving and filling the seats we don't dare in any wise offend them, and we've got to make everything smooth and soft, is not New Testament. (Sermon, "This I Believe," Toronto, 1969)

The temptation to modify the teachings of Christ with the hope that larger numbers may "accept" Him is cruelly strong in this day of speed, size, noise and crowds. But if we know what is good for us, we'll resist it with every power at our command. To yield can only result in a weak and ineffective Christianity in this generation, and death and desolation in the next. (*The Size of the Soul*, p. 119)

The crowds-at-any-price mania has taken a firm grip on American Christianity and is the motivating power back of a shockingly high percentage of all religious activity. Men and churches compete for the attention of the paying multitudes who are brought in by means of any currently popular gadget or gimmick ostensibly to have their souls saved, but, if the truth were told, often for reasons not so praiseworthy as this. (*The Size of the Soul*, p. 117)

Worship to Precede Evangelism

Listen, brethren, we can become promoters and get nowhere at all. But if we become prophets and worshipers of God, God will honor us in this awful hour in which we live. I think we ought to go to our churches and insist that we adore God. And if we can't adore Him, we ought to get purged from our sins until we can. (Sermon, "Dead Words," General Council)

Christ's Glory First

Christian believers and Christian congregations must be thoroughly consecrated to Christ's glory alone. This means absolutely turning their backs on the contemporary insistence on human glory and recognition. I have done everything I can to keep "performers" out of my pulpit. I was not called to recognize "performers." I am confident our Lord never meant for the Christian church to provide a kind of religious stage where performers proudly take their bows, seeking personal recognition. That is not God's way to an eternal work. He has never indicated that proclamation of the gospel is to be dependent on human performances. (*Tragedy in the Church: The Missing Gifts*, p. 5)

Nowadays, we perceive that even a large part of evangelical Christianity is trying to convert this world to the church. We are bringing the world in head over heels—unregenerated, uncleansed, unshriven, unbaptized, unsanctified. We are bringing the world right into the church. If we can just get some big shot to say something nice about the church, we rush into print and tell about this fellow and what nice things he said. I don't care at all about big shots because I serve a living Savior, and Jesus Christ is Lord of lords and King of kings. I believe every man ought to know this ability to see another world. (*The Tozer Pulpit*, Book 2, p. 130)

To try to get souls saved at the expense of the glory of God is to cheat God of His glory and not get souls saved anyhow. We just make proselytes who aren't Christians but something else. (Sermon, "Prayer," Chicago, 1956)

To Humble the Flesh

The methods of the Holy Ghost are pure, holy, clean methods and they're such methods as shall humble the flesh. They keep you sometimes in the state of suspension because God wants to humble you. But if you won't take the humbling and you won't wait on God then there are always methods of raising money, methods of getting things done. You can learn from TV, you can learn from Madison Avenue, you can learn it from businessmen. (Sermon, "This I Believe," Toronto, 1960)

Saved to Worship

Christ saves us to make us worshipers and workers. But we evangelicals ignore the first altogether so that we are not producing worshipers in our day. Workers, yes, we're producing workers. Founders, yes, they're a dime a dozen. Promoters, producers, artists, entertainers, religious DJs, we've got them by the thousands. Beat a bush and there will be two artists hop out and a DJ. (Sermon to Youth for Christ, National Convention of YFC in Chicago, 1960)

Christ Needs No Sponsors

Christ needs no sponsors. You know the Wheaties® approach: This ball player likes Wheaties®, therefore Wheaties® must be good. That boxer likes Wheaties®, therefore Wheaties® must be good. This movie actress likes Wheaties®, therefore Wheaties® must be good. This big politician, that chairman of the board of this company eats Wheaties®, therefore Wheaties® must be good. That's the Wheaties® approach. We have blossomed out in our day, and it's in our magazines, our religious magazines, and the philosophy is that the entertainer believes in Jesus Christ; therefore Jesus Christ must be all right. This politician believes in Jesus Christ. Why don't you accept Him? This movie actress prays to Him. Why don't you pray to Him? This playboy—this politician, this athlete, they have accepted Christ. Why don't you accept Christ? Now, that's the Wheaties® approach. Do you know what that does? That makes Jesus Christ to ride in on the sponsorship of some big shot. (Sermon to Youth for Christ, National Convention of YFC in Chicago, 1960)

We Must Have the Spirit's Power

Again, we may go astray by assuming that we can do spiritual work without spiritual power. I have heard the notion seriously advanced that whereas once to win men to Christ it was necessary to have a gift from the Holy Spirit, now religious movies make it possible for anyone to win souls, without such spiritual anointing! "Whom the gods would destroy they first make mad." Surely such a notion is madness, but until now I have not heard it challenged among the evangelicals. (*Man: The Dwelling Place of God*, p. 66)

"Help" from the World

Christ now stands in need of a patron, a celebrity who will sponsor Him before the world. He looks weakly about for some well-known figure upon whose inside popularity He can ride forth as He once rode into Jerusalem on the back of an ass's colt. His ability to draw men unto Him is frankly doubted, so He is provided with a gimmick to do the trick for Him. The cheap and tawdry glory which He once rejected is placed around His head as a crown. The crown they give Him is studded with paste imitations, all borrowed from the world: middle-class prosperity, success, fame, publicity, money, crowds, social acceptance, pomp, display, earthly honor. The lust of the flesh, the lust of the eyes and the pride of life have all been Christianized (not by the liberal, mind you, but by the evangelicals) and are now offered along with Christ to everyone who will "believe." (*God Tells the Man Who Cares*, p. 25)

To many observing persons today it appears that conversion does not do for people as much as it once did. Too often the experience passes, leaving the seeker unsatisfied and deeply disappointed. Some who are thus affected, and who are too sincere to play with religion, walk out on the whole thing and turn back frankly to the old life. Others try to make what they can out of a bad bargain and gradually adjust themselves to a modified and imperfect form of Christianity spiced up with synthetic fun and enlivened by frequent shots of stimulants in the form of "gimmick" to give it relish and sparkle. (*The Set of the Sail*, p. 18)

The flaw in current evangelism lies in its humanistic approach. It struggles to be supernaturalistic but never quite makes it. It is frankly fascinated by the great, noisy, aggressive world with its big names, its hero worship, its wealth and its garish pageantry. To the millions of disappointed persons who have always yearned for worldly glory but never attained to it, the modern evangel offers a quick and easy shortcut to their heart's desire. Peace of mind, happiness, prosperity, social acceptance, publicity, success in sports, business, the entertainment field and perchance to sit occasionally at the same banquet table with a celebrity—all this on earth and heaven at last. Certainly no insurance company can offer half as much. (*Born after Midnight*, p. 22)

God's Way, Not Ours

Why, then, are we such common Christians? Why have we settled for such shallow pleasures, those little joys that tickle the saintlets and charm the fancy of the carnal?

It is because we once heard a call to take up the cross, and instead of following toward the heights, we bargained with the Lord like a Maxwell Street huckster. We started asking selfish questions and laying down our own conditions. (*The Tozer Pulpit*, Book 8, pp. 24-25)

The new cross encourages a new and entirely different evangelistic approach. The evangelist does not demand abnegation of the old life before a new life can be received. He preaches not contrasts but similarities. He seeks to key into public interest by showing that Christianity makes no unpleasant demands; rather, it offers the same thing the world does, only on a higher level. Whatever the sin-mad world happens to be clamoring after at the moment is cleverly shown to be the very thing the gospel offers, only the religious product is better.

The new cross does not slay the sinner, it redirects him. It gears him into a cleaner and jollier way of living and saves his self-respect. To the self-assertive it says, "Come and assert yourself for Christ." To the egotist it says, "Come and do your boasting in the Lord." To the thrill seeker it says, "Come and enjoy the thrill of Christian fellowship." The Christian message is slanted in the direction of the current vogue in order to make it acceptable to the public. (*Man: The Dwelling Place of God*, p. 43)

Chapter 15

Religious Activity

It is my belief that we have just gone through a long period when Christianity was the "funniest" thing on the continent. We have been told over and over that we could have more fun serving Jesus than we could doing anything else in the whole world. It is clean, too—and we don't have a hangover!

We have been taught in some good evangelical circles, "You serve Jesus and you can have all the fun you want, and you won't have that ugly hangover!"

That was Christianity for the sake of fun, Christianity as an entertaining medium. The whole thing is offensive and foul before God Almighty. My brother, the cross of Christ isn't fun, and it never was fun.

There is such a thing as the joy of the Lord which is the strength of His people; there is such a thing as having joy unspeakable and full of glory, but the idea that Christianity is another form of entertainment is perfectly ridiculous.

When I sing "Amazing Grace, How Sweet the Sound," I am worshiping God Almighty. If you want to call "entertainment" that which they do before the throne when they cry day and night without ceasing, "Holy, holy, holy, Lord God Almighty," then I am an entertainer. If it isn't entertainment—and it isn't—then I am a worshiper.

The Church must worship, beloved! There is more healing joy in five minutes of worship than there is in five nights of revelry. Nobody ever worshiped God and went out and committed suicide as a hangover. Many a man has killed himself because he had just burned himself out trying to have fun. Many a pretty young woman has thrown herself into having fun, and before she is twenty-five, she has to have a retread job done on her countenance—she has simply burned herself out. (*The Tozer Pulpit*, Book 2, pp. 18-19)

Consider God

We may live out a full lifetime and die without once having our minds challenged by the sweet mystery of the Godhead if we depend upon the churches to do the challenging. They are altogether too busy playing with shadows and getting "adjusted" to one thing and another to spend much time thinking about God. It might be well, therefore, to consider for a moment longer the divine inscrutability. (*The Divine Conquest*, pp. 94-95)

I am encouraged to believe that you are not satisfied with religious toys but that you actually come to church to gear into deity and meet God and hear from the world above. (Sermon, "In the Beginning," Chicago)

The World's Amusements

I date back to the time when the holiness people and the full gospel people and the Alliance people believed that the amusements of the world were not for Christians. And so it was understood that when you got converted and got filled with the Spirit you gave up the world's amusements. Then there was a slow change and, in the name of fundamental Christianity, one by one we met those worldly amusements at the door and sprinkled them with holy water. And nobody is against them anymore. We now advertise them and they are part of our structure.

"Muse" means to think and "amuse" means not to think. That little "a" on there makes it negative. A fellow says, "Sometimes I sit on my front porch and think and other times I just sit on my front porch." The man who sits on his front porch and thinks is musing, but the man just who sits on his front porch has to be amused. That is, he has to see something or hear something to keep him from collapsing. And so the devil has invented the amusements to keep us from collapsing.

You say, "What are these amusements?" I shouldn't name them for the reason there is no fixed rule about it. Christians are not alike; they are different from each other and therefore what would be to one an amusement that hinders would not hinder another. So the rule must be, if they encumber me, if they will cause me to lose I will lay them aside.

Some people can't drink coffee because it keeps them awake. But I can drink a cup of coffee and lie down as if I were drugged. I don't have that problem, so what to them would be a hindrance isn't to me a hindrance. . . . What is hindering you might not hinder me. And what hinders me might not hinder you. So everybody has to find out for himself, "What am I doing by way of amusements? What am I indulging in that hinders me?" And then, don't defend yourself and find an argument but lay it off. (Sermon #39 on Hebrews, Toronto)

The idea that this world is a playground instead of a battleground has now been accepted in practice by the vast majority of fundamentalist Christians. They might hedge around the question if they were asked bluntly to declare their position, but their conduct gives them away. They are facing both ways, enjoying Christ and the world, gleefully telling everyone that accepting Jesus does not require them to give up their fun—Christianity is just the jolliest thing imaginable. The "worship" growing out of such a view of life is as far off center as the view itself—a sort of sanctified nightclub without the champagne and the dressed-up drunks. (*This World: Playground or Battleground?*, p. 6)

Entertainment Easier than Instruction

A religious mentality characterized by timidity and lack of moral courage has given us today a flabby Christianity, intellectually impoverished, dull, repetitious and, to a great many persons, just plain boresome. This is peddled as the very faith of our fathers in direct lineal descent from Christ and the apostles. We spoon-feed this insipid pablum to our inquiring youth and, to make it palatable, spice it up with carnal amusements filched from the unbelieving world. It is easier to entertain than to instruct, it is easier to follow degenerate public taste than to think for oneself, so too many of our evangelical leaders let their minds atrophy while they keep their fingers nimble operating religious gimmicks to bring in the curious crowds. (*God Tells the Man Who Cares*, p. 103)

The Religious Game

By observing the ways of men at play I have been able to understand better the ways of men at prayer. Most men, indeed, play at religion as they play at games, religion itself being of all games the one most universally played. The various sports have their rules and their balls and their players; the game excites interest, gives pleasure and consumes time, and when it is over the competing teams laugh and leave the field. It is common to see a player leave one team and join another and a few days later play against their old mates with as great zest as he formerly displayed when playing for them. The whole thing is arbitrary. It consists in solving artificial problems and attacking difficulties which have been deliberately created for the sake of the game. It has no moral roots and is not supposed to have. No one is the better for his self-imposed toil. It is all but a pleasant activity which changes nothing and settles nothing at last.

If the conditions we describe were confined to the ballpark we might pass it over without further thought, but what are we to say when this same spirit enters the sanctuary and decides the attitude of men toward God and religion? For the Church has also its fields and its rules and its equipment for playing the game of pious words. It has its devotees, both laymen and professionals, who support the game with their money and encourage it with their presence, but who are no different in life or character from many who take in religion no interest at all.

As an athlete uses a ball so do many of us use words: words spoken and words sung, words written and words uttered in prayer. We throw them swiftly across the field; we learn to handle them with dexterity and grace; we build reputations upon our word-skill and gain as our reward the applause of those who have enjoyed the game. But the emptiness of it is apparent from the fact that after the pleasant religious game no one is basically any different from what he had been before. The bases of life remain unchanged, the same old principles govern, the same old Adam rules. (*God's Pursuit of Man*, p. 32)

Christ calls men to carry a cross; we call them to have fun in His name. He calls them to forsake the world; we assure them that if they but accept Jesus the world is their oyster. He calls them to suffer; we call them to enjoy all the bourgeois comforts modern civilization affords. He calls them to self-abnegation and death. We call them to spread themselves like green bay trees or perchance even to become stars in a pitiful fifth-rate religious zodiac. He calls them to holiness; we call them to a cheap and tawdry happiness that would have been rejected with scorn by the least of the Stoic philosophers. (*Warfare of the Spirit*, pp. 83-84)

Break with the World's Ways

We must have a new reformation. There must come a violent break with that irresponsible, amusement-mad, paganized pseudo-religion which passes today for the faith of Christ and which is being spread all over the world by unspiritual men employing unscriptural methods to achieve their ends. (*The Root of the Righteous*, p. 110)

Modern churches have made fun a symbol of their religion. I want to grieve, bury my head in my hands and sob before God when I hear, as I often do, precious young people whom I would give my blood for, get up and in a little tiny voice say, "Oh, I am so glad I have found out that you do not have to be a sinner to have fun. We have fun in the church, too. You can follow Jesus and have fun." Then they sit down. How they have been betrayed! It is the cross that is the symbol of the Christian life. But we will not pick up our crosses. We will not forgive our enemies. We will not be reconciled. (*Rut, Rot or Revival*, p. 148)

Is it not a strange thing and a wonder that, with the shadow of atomic destruction hanging over the world and with the coming of Christ drawing near, the professed followers of the Lord should be giving themselves up to religious amusements? That in an hour when mature saints are so desperately needed, vast numbers of believers should revert to spiritual childhood and clamor for religious toys? (*The Root of the Righteous*, p. 33)

Our Lord died an apparent failure, discredited by the leaders of established religion, rejected by society and forsaken by His friends. The man who ordered Him to the cross was the successful statesman whose hand the ambitious hack politician kissed. It took the resurrection to demonstrate how gloriously Christ had triumphed and how tragically the governor had failed.

Yet today the professed church seems to have learned nothing. We are still seeing as men see and judging after the manner of man's judgment. How much eager-beaver religious work is done out of a carnal desire to make good. How many hours of prayer are wasted beseeching God to bless projects that are geared to the glorification of little men. How much sacred money is poured out upon men who, in spite of their tear-in-the-voice appeals, nevertheless seek only to make a fair show in the flesh. (*Born after Midnight*, p. 58)

Apathy and Activity in Faith

In only one field of human interest are we slow and apathetic: That is the field of personal religion. There, for some strange reason, our enthusiasm lags. Church people habitually approach the matter of their personal relation to God in a dull, half-hearted way which is altogether out of keeping with their general temperament and wholly inconsistent with the importance of the subject.

It is true that there is a lot of religious activity among us. Interchurch basketball tournaments, religious splash parties followed by devotions, weekend camping trips with a Bible quiz around the fire, Sunday school picnics, building fund drives and ministerial breakfasts are with us in unbelievable numbers, and they are carried on with typical American gusto. It is when we enter the sacred precincts of the heart's personal religion that we suddenly lose all enthusiasm. (*Of God and Men*, p. 8)

The churches try to dispel their gloomy mood by a number of methods. One of them is by multiplying activities. We're just so active, we Christians, we run in circles and chase each other around until you just look up anywhere and see the back of a good saintly brother's neck on his way going somewhere or coming from somewhere. We try to dispel our deep unhappiness by being very active but the fact is it doesn't work. Or we try to do it by the introduction of religious fun. That's been our method in the last few years—instead of having a victorious inward life we have a defeated heavy inward life and they can only keep from breaking down and having a crying time by having religious entertainment. (Sermon, "Epistle to Torontonians," Toronto, 1960)

Too Much Activity

If there is no God in their eyes then, they get something else in their eyes. If they do not enjoy worshiping the great God Almighty who made them, then they find something else. If you had a list of all the things that people have thought out to do to satisfy themselves, to get some pleasure out of living, it would fill a good size book and then it wouldn't be all. ("The Chief End of Man," Sermon #2, Toronto, 1962)

We are purveying tranquility now, selling it like soap and asking our people in the name of John 3:16 to come and get tranquilized. And so we have a tranquilized Church that is enjoying herself immensely at her banquets and her times of fun and her coffee clutches and her fellowships. And then she is singing about the Word of the Lord that's like a flower garden. (Sermon, "Doctrine of the Remnant," Chicago, 1957)

We are running our churches the way you would run a club. I wish we might get back again to worship so that when people come into the church they sense instantly that they are among holy people and fall on their faces and worship God. ("The Chief End of Man," Sermon #4, Toronto, 1962)

Religious "activists" have many things of which they can boast. They build churches. They write hymns and books. Musically, they sing and play. Some of them will take time to engage in prayer. Others will organize movements and crusades and campaigns. But no matter how early in the morning they begin and no matter how late at night they stay with their projects, if it is an exercise of human talent for religious purposes, it can only wind up as a mortal brain doing a mortal job. And across it God will write a superscription: "It came to die, and it came to go!" (*Tragedy in the Church: the Missing Gifts*, p. 31)

Noise Is Not Necessarily Worship

I don't believe that it is always true that we are worshiping God when we are making a lot of racket. Religious racket and worship don't necessarily mean the same thing. Also, I want to warn you cultured, quiet, self-possessed, poised, sophisticated people that if you are so sure of yourself that it embarrasses you if anybody says "amen," you got some help coming to you. The people of God always were a little bit noisy. ("The Chief End of Man," Sermon # 41, Toronto, 1962)

"The accent in the Church today," says Leonard Ravenhill, the English evangelist, "is not on devotion, but on commotion." Religious extroversion has been carried to such an extreme in evangelical circles that hardly anyone has the desire, to say nothing of the courage, to question the soundness of it. Externalism has taken over. God now speaks by the wind and the earthquake only; the still small voice can be heard no more. The whole religious machine has become a noisemaker. The adolescent taste which loves the loud horn and thundering exhaust has gotten into the activities of modern Christians. The old question, "What is the chief end of man?" is now answered, "To dash about the world and add to the din thereof." And all this is done in the name of Him who did not strive, nor cry, nor make His voice to be heard in the streets (Matthew 12:18-21). (*The Root of the Righteous*, p. 75)

Don't Forget the Spirit

You may think it out of place for me to say so, but in our churches today we are leaning too heavily upon human talents and educated abilities. We forget that the illumination of the Holy Spirit of God is a necessity, not only in our ministerial preparation, but in the administrative and leadership functions of our churches. (*Jesus Is Victor*, p. 48)

Some of these attractions that we have to win people and keep them coming may be fine or they may be cheap, they may be elevated or they may be degrading. They may be artistic or they may be coarse—it all depends upon who is running the show! But the Holy Spirit is not the center of attraction, and the Lord is not the one who is in charge. We bring in all sorts of antiscriptural and unscriptural claptrap to keep the people happy and keep them coming.

As I see it, the great woe is not the presence of these religious toys and trifles—but the fact that they have become a necessity, and the presence of the Eternal Spirit is not in our midst! (*The Tozer Pulpit*, Book 2, pp. 40-41)

The Church in the Media

There has probably never been another time in the history of the world when so many people knew so much about religious happenings as they do today. The newspapers are eager to print religious news; the secular news magazines devote several pages of each issue to the doings of the church and the synagogue; a number of press associations gather church news and make it available to the religious journals at a small cost. Even the hiring of professional publicity men to plug one or another preacher or religious movement is no longer uncommon; the mails are stuffed with circulars and "releases," while radio and television join to tell the listening public what religious people are doing throughout the world.

Greater publicity for religion may be well and I have no fault to find with it. Surely religion should be the most newsworthy thing on earth, and there may be some small encouragement in the thought that vast numbers of persons want to read about it. What disturbs me is that amidst all the religious hubbub hardly a voice is raised to tell us what God thinks about the whole thing. (*Of God and Men*, p. 21)

The Craze for Activity

I still believe, however, that if someone should come along who could make himself heard to thousands instead of to a few hundred, someone with as much oil as intellect and as much power as penetration, we could yet save evangelical Christianity from the dead-end street in which she finds herself. I warn you—don't for one second let the crowds, the bustle of religious activity, a surge of religious thinking—fool you into thinking that there is a lot of spirituality. It isn't so. (*The Tozer Pulpit*, Book 3, p. 34)

Actually, our craze for activity brings few enriching benefits into our Christian circles. If you look into our churches, you will find groups of half-saved, half-sanctified, carnal people who know more about social niceties than they do about the New Testament; and more about love stories and soap operas than they do about the Holy Spirit. (*The Tozer Pulpit*, Book 4, p. 136)

We would make a clear distinction here between moral action and mere religious activity. In truth there is already too much of that popular type of activity which does little more than agitate the surface of religion. Its never-ending squirrel-cage motion gives the impression that much is being done, when actually nothing really important is happening and no genuine spiritual progress is being made. From such we must turn away. (*We Travel an Appointed Way*, p. 77)

In an effort to get the work of the Lord done we often lose contact with the Lord of the work and quite literally wear our people out as well. I have heard more than one pastor boast that his church was a "live" one, pointing to the printed calendar as proof—something on every night and several meetings during the day. Of course this proves nothing except that the pastor and the church are being guided by a bad spiritual philosophy. A great many of these time-consuming activities are useless and others plain ridiculous. "But," say the eager-beavers who run the religious squirrel cages, "they provide fellowship and they hold our people together."

To this I reply that what they provide is not fellowship at all, and if that is the best thing the church has to offer to hold the people together, it is not a Christian church in the New Testament meaning of that word. The center of attraction in a true church is the Lord Jesus Christ. As for fellowship, let the Holy Spirit define it for us: "And they continued steadfastly in the apostles' doctrine and fellowship, and in breaking of bread, and in prayers" (Acts 2:42). (*That Incredible Christian*, p. 136)

The Directionless Church

Lack of direction is the cause of many tragic failures in religious activities. The churches are overrun with persons of both sexes (though the vast majority are men) who have never known a clear call of God to anything in particular. Such people are often victims of whim and chance, the easy prey of ambitious leaders who seek to gain prominence by using others for their own ends. The directionless Christian is the one who supports the new and spectacular, regardless of whether or not it is in accord with the Scriptures and the revealed will of God. (*This World: Playground or Battleground?*, p. 55)

So we find this strange and contradictory situation: a world of noisy, headlong religious activity carried on without moral energy or spiritual fervor. In a year's travel among the churches one scarcely finds a believer whose blood count is normal and whose temperature is up to standard. The flush and excitement of the soul in love must be sought in the New Testament or in the biographies of the saints; we look for them in vain among the professed followers of Christ in our day. (*The Price of Neglect*, p. 26)

Were the church a pure and Spirit-filled body, wholly led and directed by spiritual considerations, certainly the purest and the saintliest men and women would be the ones most appreciated and most honored; but the opposite is true. Godliness is no longer valued, except for the very old or the very dead. The saintly souls are forgotten in the whirl of religious activity. The noisy, the self-assertive, the entertaining are sought after and rewarded in every way, with gifts, crowds, offerings and publicity. The Christlike, the self-forgetting, the other-worldly are jostled aside to make room for the latest con- verted playboy who is usually not too well con- verted and still very much a playboy. (*Man: The Dwelling Place of God*, pp. 97-98)

Change with the Times?

Any evangelism which by appeal to common interests and chatter about current events seeks to establish a common ground where the sinner can feel at home is as false as the altars of Baal ever were. Every effort to smooth out the road for men and to take away the guilt and the embarrassment is worse than wasted; it is evil and dangerous to the souls of men.

One of the most popular current errors, and the one out of which springs most of the noisy, blus- tering religious activity being carried on in evangelical circles these days, is the notion that as times change the church must change with them. Christians must adapt their methods by the demands of the people. If they want ten-minute sermons, give them ten-minute sermons. If they want truth in capsule form, give it to them. If they want pictures, give them plenty of pictures. If they like stories, tell them stories. If they prefer to absorb their religious instruction through the drama, go along with them—give them what they want. "The message is the same, only the method changes," say the advocates of compromise.

"Whom the gods would destroy they first make mad," the old Greeks said, and they were wiser than they knew. That mentality which mistakes Sodom for Jerusalem and Hollywood for the Holy City is too gravely astray to be explained otherwise than as a judicial madness visited upon professed Christians for affronts committed against the Spirit of God. "Hear ye indeed, but understand not; and see ye indeed, but perceive not. Make the heart of this people fat, and make their ears heavy, and shut their eyes; lest they see with their eyes, and hear with their ears, and understand with their heart, and convert, and be healed" (Isaiah 6:9-10). (*God Tells the Man Who Cares*, pp. 18-19)

Chapter 16

Worldliness

Low Spirituality

Within the last quarter of a century we have actually seen a major shift in the beliefs and practices of the evangelical wing of the church so radical as to amount to a complete sellout; and all this behind the cloak of fervent orthodoxy. With Bibles under their arms and bundles of tracts in their pockets, religious persons now meet to carry on "services" so carnal, so pagan that they can hardly be distinguished from the old vaudeville shows of earlier days. And for a preacher or writer to challenge this heresy is to invite ridicule and abuse from every quarter. (*Of God and Men*, p. 17)

Influenced by Hollywood

I don't like to say this, but I think that some of you may not be ready for this message because you are more influenced by the world than you are by the New Testament. I am perfectly certain that I could rake up fifteen boxcar loads of fundamentalist Christians this hour in the city of Chicago who are more influenced in their whole outlook by Hollywood than they are by the Lord Jesus Christ. I am positive that much that passes for the gospel in our day is very little more than a very mild case of orthodox religion grafted on to a heart that is sold out to the world in its pleasures and tastes and ambitions. (*How to Be Filled with the Holy Spirit*, p. 26)

There are those who are more influenced by the world than by the New Testament, and they are not ready for the Holy Spirit.

Of these people, we have to say that they are influenced far more by Hollywood than they are by Jerusalem. Their spirit and mode of life is more like Hollywood than it is like Jerusalem. If you were to suddenly set them down in the New Jerusalem, they would not feel at home because their mode, the texture of their mind, has been created for them by twentieth century entertainment and not by the things of God! (*The Tozer Pulpit*, Book 2, p. 110)

Aside from a few of the grosser sins, the sins of the unregenerated world are now approved by a shocking number of professedly "born-again" Christians and copied eagerly. Young Christians take as their models the rankest kind of worldlings and try to be as much like them as possible. Religious leaders have adopted the techniques of the advertisers; boasting, baiting and shameless exaggerating are now carried on as a normal procedure in church work. The moral climate is not that of the New Testament, but that of Hollywood and Broadway. (*Keys to the Deeper Life*, p. 22)

Popular evangelicalism has been selling out to the worldly spirit and worldly methods to a point where Hollywood now has more influence than Jerusalem ever had. Youth take for their examples not the saints of old but the stars of today. The chaste dignity and sparkling purity of true Christianity has been displaced by a cheap hillbillyism wholly unworthy of our Lord Jesus Christ. (*Keys to the Deeper Life*, p. 89)

The evangelical Church is oriented around showmanship. I can always tell a showman. I smile to myself and pray that God will wake him up when I hear a young man leap to the platform as in schools and tent meetings and other places. He leaps up just vibrating. He's an "MC." He learned that from TV and he knows how to do it. He smiles that greasy smile that they put on with paddles and he drags that damnable thing into the church and leaps up and announces a meeting. "Now, Jim Smith, Mabel Persnickety and Harry Jones will sing. All right, kids."

I know where he's been and I sniff no myrrh, no aloes, no cassia, no fragrance of heaven. I smell—I know where he's been. His orientation is TV and movies. But, he's got a Bible as big as a cedar chest under his arm and he carries it down the road, and says, "I'm preaching a sermon five blocks long." Then he upsets his sermon as soon as he arrives at church by acting like a worldling. (Sermon, "Doctrine of the Remnant," Chicago, 1957)

Watered Down Christianity

I wonder if you realize that in many ways the preaching of the Word of God is being pulled down to the level of the ignorant and spiritually obtuse; that we must tell stories and jokes and entertain and amuse in order to have a few people in the audience? We do these things that we may have some reputation and that there may be money in the treasury to meet the church bills.

I believe in being honest about it—let's admit that we have to pull down the application of the gospel not to the standard of the one who is really thirsting after God, but to the one who is the most carnal, the cheapest saintling hanging on by the teeth anywhere in the kingdom of God!

In many churches Christianity has been watered down until the solution is so weak that if it were poison it would not hurt anyone, and if it were medicine it would not cure anyone! (*The Tozer Pulpit*, Book 8, p. 12)

A Pitiful Hybrid

It is no more than a religious platitude to say that the trouble with us today is that we have tried to bridge the gulf between two opposites, the

world and the Church, and have performed an il-
licit marriage for which there is no biblical authority. Actually no real union between the world
and the Church is possible. When the Church
joins up with the world it is the true Church no
longer but only a pitiful hybrid thing, an object of
smiling contempt to the world and an abomination to the Lord. (*God's Pursuit of Man*, p. 120)

Worldly Churches

We have become in our day the greatest bunch
of sacrilegious jokesters in the world. I have seen
pictures in the paper of people who thought is was
a very humourous thing to show a little spotted
dog with his paws crossed and his eyes shut, bow-
ing his head as if in prayer.

The Bible says, "Beware of dogs," and I might
add: "Beware of the fools who teach dogs to
pray." (*The Tozer Pulpit*, Book 1, p. 106)

Evangelical Christianity, at least in the United
States, is now tragically below the New Testament standard. Worldliness is an accepted part of
our way of life. Our religious mood is social instead of spiritual. We have lost the art of worship.
We are not producing saints. Our models are successful businessmen, celebrated athletes and theatrical personalities. We carry on our religious
activities after the methods of the modern advertiser. Our homes have been turned into theaters.
Our literature is shallow and our hymnody bor-

ders on sacrilege. And scarcely anyone appears to care. (*Warfare of the Spirit*, p. 138)

Evangelical Christianity is fast becoming the religion of the bourgeoisie. The well-to-do, the upper-middle classes, the politically prominent, the celebrities are accepting our religion by the thousands and parking their expensive cars outside our church doors, to the uncontrollable glee of our religious leaders who seem completely blind to the fact that the vast majority of these new patrons of the Lord of glory have not altered their moral habits in the slightest nor given any evidence of true conversion that would have been accepted by the saintly fathers who built the churches. (*Warfare of the Spirit*, p. 16)

The real peril today arises from within the fold of orthodox believers. It consists of an acceptance of the world's values, a belief that the kingdoms of the world and the glory of them are valid prizes to be pursued by believing men and women. Blind leaders of blind souls are admitting that there is something to be said in favor of the world-glory after all; they insist that Christians should not cut themselves off from the pleasures of the world, except, of course, from those that are too degraded for respectable society. Everything else goes, and the very values that Christ scorned are now being used to attract people to the gospel. (*God Tells the Man Who Cares*, p. 24)

Results of Ignoring the Spirit

When the Holy Spirit is ignored or rejected, religious people are forced either to do their own creating or to fossilize completely. A few churches accept fossilization as the will of God and settle down to the work of preserving their past—as if it needed preserving. Others seek to appear modern and to imitate the current activities of the world with the mistaken idea that they are being creative. And after a fashion they are, but the creatures of their creative skill are sure to be toys and trifles, mere imitations of the world and altogether lacking in the qualities of eternity—holiness and spiritual dignity. The hallmark of the Holy Spirit is not there. (*This World: Playground or Battleground?*, p. 37)

Religion Gone Glamorous

The mania after glamor and the contempt of the ordinary are signs and portents in American society. Even religion has gone glamorous. And in case you do not know what glamor is, I might explain that it is a compound of sex, paint, padding and artificial lights. It came to America by way of the honky-tonk and the movie lot, got accepted by the world first and then strutted into the church—vain, self-admiring and contemptuous. Instead of the Spirit of God in our midst, we now have the spirit of glamor, as artificial as painted death and as hollow as the skull, which is its symbol. (*This World: Playground or Battleground?*, p. 94)

But let us be more specific. About whom am I
speaking here? The liberal who denies the authen-
ticity of the Scriptures? I wish it were so. No, I
write off the liberal as long dead and expect nothing from him. It is of the evangelical church that I
speak, and of the so-called gospel churches. I speak
of the theology of popular evangelism which
quotes the Bible copiously but without one trace of
authority, accepts the world at its own estimate,
chides sinners like a weak-chinned father of a fam-
ily who has long ago lost control of his household
and doesn't expect to be obeyed, offers Christ as a
religious tranquilizer who is without sovereignty
and without any semblance of Lordship, adopts
the world's methods, courts the favor of rich men,
politicians and playboys—with the understanding,
of course, that the said playboy will stoop to say a
nice word about Jesus now and then.

I refer to a religious journalism ostensibly orthodox but which can scarcely be told in appearance, tone, spirit, language, method or aim from
the secular magazine it so sedulously apes. I refer
to the Christianity which says to Christ, "We will
eat our own bread, and wear our own apparel:
only let us be called by thy name, to take away
our reproach" (Isaiah 4:1). I refer to the masses of
Christians who have "accepted" Jesus, but who
turn their churches into playhouses, are entirely
ignorant of worship, misunderstand the cross and
are totally blind to the serious implications of discipleship. (*God Tells the Man Who Cares*, p. 37)

The present flair for religion has not made people heavenly minded; rather it has secularized religion and put its approval upon the carnal values of fallen men. It glorifies success and eagerly prints religious testimonies from big corporation tycoons, actors, athletes, politicians and very important persons of every kind regardless of their reputation or lack of one. Religion is promoted by the identical technique used to sell cigarettes. You pray to soothe your nerves just as you smoke to regard your composure after a sharp business transaction or a tight athletic contest. Books are written by the scores to show that Jesus is a regular fellow and Christianity a wise use of the highest psychological laws. All the holy principles of the Sermon on the Mount are present in reverse. Not the meek are blessed, but the self-important; not they who mourn but they who smile and smile and smile. Not the poor in spirit are dear to God, but they who are accounted somebody by the secular press. Not they that hunger and thirst after righteousness are filled, but they that hunger for publicity. (*The Price of Neglect*, p. 100)

Too Often Strangers

To come to our devotions straight from carnal or worldly interests is to make it impossible to relish the deep, sweet thoughts found in the great books we are discussing here. We must know their heart-language, must vibrate in harmony with them, must share their inward experiences or they will mean nothing to us. Because we are too often strangers to their spiritual mood, we are unable to profit by them and are forced to turn to one or another form of religious entertainment to make our Christianity palatable enough to endure. (*The Size of the Soul*, p. 49)

The Scramble for Popularity

Christianity's scramble for popularity today is an unconscious acknowledgment of spiritual decline. Her eager fawning at the feet of the world's great is a grief to the Holy Spirit and an embarrassment to the sons of God. The lick-spittle attitude of popular Christian leaders toward the world's celebrities would make such men as Elijah or George Fox sick to the stomach. (*The Next Chapter after the Last*, p. 21)

The secular press, which of course is always quick to sense trends and give the public what it wants, has found that religion is news. A sufficiently large number of those who buy newspapers and magazines are interested enough in religion to make it profitable to print increasingly generous amounts of religious copy. Religious books are among the best sellers. Prominent people are telling the world what they believe. Religion is woven into sports, politics, the theater. It is frequently a part of nightclub chatter, and the radio and TV comedian has learned that a serious word about prayer and churchgoing at the end of his routine will please most of his listeners. (*The Price of Neglect*, p. 82)

Christians have fallen into the habit of accepting the noisiest and most notorious among them as the best and the greatest. They too have learned to equate popularity with excellence, and in open defiance of the Sermon on the Mount they have given their approval not to the meek but to the self-assertive; not to the mourner but to the self-assured; not to the pure in heart who see God but to the publicity hunter who seeks headlines. (*Man: The Dwelling Place of God*, p. 96)

Inner Loneliness

Where God is not known in the inner shrine, the individual must try to compensate for his sense of aloneness in whatever way he can. Most persons rush away to the world to find companionship and surround themselves with every kind of diversionary activity. All devices for killing time, every shallow scheme for entertainment, are born out of this inner loneliness. It is a significant and revealing fact that such things have in these last days grown into billion dollar enterprises! So much will men pay to forget that they are a temple without a God, a garden where no voice is heard in the cool of the day. (*The Next Chapter after the Last*, p. 104)

The World's Methods or God's?

Many evangelical leaders lack historic perspective and thus do not know how the Holy Spirit has worked and how He works. We lack the knowledge of God's ways and so we substitute our own. There are three methods that are being introduced in our time which are contrary to and diametrically opposed to the methods of the New Testament. One, the methods of big business. The second the method of show business. And the third, the method of the Madison Avenue advertiser. And Bible methods are supplemented and the Holy Spirit is grieved and withdraws Himself; and we, because we are young and have a lot of animal spirits, we make up by sheer enthusiasm what we lack in the power of the Spirit, and because we lack historic perspective and spiritual discernment we don't know one for the other. Bible methods are supplanted. You can be sure of this—that to attempt to carry on a sacred, holy work, such as the work of the Church of Christ and of evangelism and of missionary activities around the world after the methods of big business and show business and the Madison Avenue advertiser is to grieve the Holy Ghost and remain in Babylonian captivity. (Sermon to Youth for Christ, National Convention of YFC, Chicago)

The Church has sprung a leak and the world is leaking into the Church. (Sermon to Youth for Christ, National Convention of YFC, Chicago)

Called to Separation

We believe that we are called to separation. We are called to separate from the world's follies and the world's pleasures and the world's ways and the world's values and the world's ambitions and the world's greed and the world's vices and the world's habits. There is a sharp moral antithesis which exists between the Church and the world and this can never be reconciled. It effects every Christian so that the Christian sins when he fraternizes with the world. He grieves the Holy Spirit by worldly living and stunts his spiritual growth by imitating the world. (Sermon, "Christian Manifesto," Toronto, 1960)

We are against the unhappy and unholy importation into Christian circles and worship at any cost. We're against the strange fires which are being offered on the altars of the Lord. We are against the strange sacrifices which they are offering. We are against the strange gods in our sanctuaries and we're especially against the baptized foolery and sanctified frivolity that is taking over fundamentalism. (Sermon, "Christian Manifesto," Toronto, 1960)

As soon as you try to turn the flock everybody says you're against everything. Of course, I'm against the devil, I'm against sin, I'm against worldliness, I'm against the flesh and I'm against Christianity that pretends to be Christianity and isn't. I'm against spiritual ignorance that tries to harmonize Christianity with the world. It's absolutely futile to try to do it.

There was a day when our religious leaders were made fun of and laughed at and opposed, even put in jail and driven out of town, but nowadays they are riding on the shoulders of the mobs and the multitudes because they are trying to make Christianity as much like the world as possible in order to win the world. That's the philosophy of the present hour—trying to make Christianity like the world. Show them it's like them only it's a little higher, and pretty soon you'll win them. Don't we know that Christianity demands the impossible and secures it? Don't we know that Christianity cuts straight across the instincts of man? Don't we know that the message of Jesus Christ runs contrary to man and not in favor of man? (Sermon, "Contradictions," Chicago)

A Longing after God

I would rather die, I would rather walk out here on the sidewalk and drop over and be gathered up by the authorities and carried away than to lose my receptivity and lose my hunger and lose my discontent with my present state. I grieve over the playboy preachers and the happy back-slapping fellows who think that Jesus Christ is simply wonderful. But there is no receptivity of God, no longing after God, no deep yearning for holiness, no inner hunger to be like Jesus. (Sermon, "Marks of the Elect," Toronto)

Every church should see to it that its methods praise God. No matter how skillfully we praise God musically, if our methods are not praiseful, then we are not praising God really. We should

see that our pulpit praises God. (Tozer's last sermon in Chicago, 1959)

Puddles of Godliness

The evangelical church is just vanity fair.
There are little puddles of godliness lying here
and there but no rivers of godliness, just little
puddles and most of them have wiggle worms in
them and few toads around the edges. Just puddles. God wants us to have rivers and the reason
we don't have rivers is we are not hearing the
right voice. It's just vanity fair religion. Men promote themselves without shame today. (Sermon,
"He Must Increase," General Council)

Chapter 17

Editor's note: This booklet was probably published sometime in the mid 1950s.

The Menace of the Religious Movie

When God gave to Moses the blueprint of the Tabernacle He was careful to include every detail; then, lest Moses should get the notion that he could improve on the original plan, God warned him solemnly, "And look that thou make them after their pattern which was shewed thee in the mount" (Exodus 25:40). God, not Moses, was the architect. To decide the plan was the prerogative of the Deity. No one dare alter it so much as a hairbreadth.

The New Testament Church also is built after a pattern. Not the doctrines only, but the methods are divinely given. The doctrines are expressly stated in so many words. Some of the methods followed by the early New Testament Church had been given by direct command; others were used by God's specific approval, having obviously been commanded the apostles by the Spirit. The point is that when the New Testament canon was closed the blueprint for the age was complete. God has added nothing since that time.

From God's revealed plan we depart at our peril. Every departure has two consequences, the immediate and the remote. The immediate touches the individual and those close to him; the remote extends into the future to unknown times and may expand so far as to influence for evil the whole Church of God on earth.

The temptation to introduce "new" things into the work of God has always been too strong for some people to resist. The Church has suffered untold injury at the hands of well intentioned but misguided persons who have felt that they know more about running God's work than Christ and His apostles did. A solid train of boxcars would not suffice to haul away the religious truck which has been brought into the service of the Church with the hope of improving on the original pattern. These things have been, one and all, positive hindrances to the progress of the Truth and have so altered the divinely planned structure that the apostles, were they to return to earth today, would scarcely recognize the misshapen thing which has resulted.

Our Lord while on earth cleansed the Temple, and periodic cleansings have been necessary in the Church of God throughout the centuries. Every generation is sure to have its ambitious amateur to come up with some shiny gadget which he proceeds to urge upon the priests before the altar. That the Scriptures do not justify its existence does not seem to bother him at all. It is brought in anyway and presented in the very name of orthodoxy. Soon it is identified in the minds of the Christian public with all that is good and holy. Then, of course, to attack the gadget is to attack the Truth itself. This is an old familiar technique so often and so long practiced by the devotees of error that I marvel how the children of God can be taken in by it.

We of the evangelical faith are in the rather awkward position of criticizing Roman Catholicism for its weight of unscriptural impedimenta and at the same time tolerating in our own churches a world of religious fribble as bad as holy water or the elevated host. Heresy of method may be as deadly as heresy of message. Old-line Protestantism has long ago been smothered to death by extra-scriptural rubbish. Unless we of the gospel churches wake up soon we shall most surely die by the same means.

Within the last few years a new method has been invented for imparting spiritual knowledge; or, to be more accurate, it is not new at all, but is an adaptation of a gadget of some years standing, one which by its origin and background belongs not to the Church but to the world. Some within the fold of the Church have thrown their mantle over it, have "blessed it with a text" and are now trying to show that it is the very gift of God for our day. But however eloquent the sales talk, it is an unauthorized addition nevertheless, and was never a part of the pattern shown us on the mount.

I refer, of course, to the religious movie.

For the motion picture as such I have no irrational allergy. It is a mechanical invention merely and is in its essence amoral; that is, it is neither good nor bad, but neutral. With any physical object or any creature lacking the power of choice it could not be otherwise. Whether such an object is useful or harmful depends altogether upon who uses it and what he uses it for. No moral quality attaches where there is no free choice. Sin and righteousness lie in the will. The motion picture is in the same class as the automobile, the typewriter or the radio: a powerful instrument for good or evil, depending upon how it is applied.

For teaching the facts of physical science the motion picture has been useful. The public schools have used it successfully to teach health habits to children. The army employed it to speed up instruction during the war. That it has been of real service within its limited field is freely acknowledged here.

Over against this is the fact that the motion picture in evil hands has been a source of moral corruption to millions. No one who values his reputation as a responsible adult will deny that the sex movie and the crime movie have done untold injury to the lives of countless young people in our generation. The harm lies not in the instrument itself, but in the evil will of those who use it for their own selfish ends.

I am convinced that the modern religious movie is an example of the harmful misuse of a neutral instrument. There are sound reasons for my belief. I am prepared to state them.

That I may be as clear as possible, let me explain what I do and do not mean by the religious movie. I do not mean the missionary picture nor the travel picture which aims to focus attention upon one or another section of the world's great harvest field. These do not come under discussion and will be left entirely out of consideration here.

By the religious movie I mean that type of motion picture which attempts to treat spiritual themes by dramatic representation. These are (as their advocates dare not deny) frank imitations of the authentic Hollywood variety, but the truth requires me to say that they are infinitely below their models, being mostly awkward, amateurish and, from an artistic standpoint, hopelessly and piteously bad.

These pictures are produced by *acting* a religious story before the camera. Take for example the famous and beautiful story of the Prodigal Son. This would be made into a movie by treating the narrative as a scenario. Stage scenery would be set up, actors would take the roles of father, prodigal son, elder brother, etc. There would be a plot, sequence and dramatic denouement as in the ordinary tearjerker shown at the Bijou movie house on Main Street in any one of a thousand American towns. The story would be acted out, photographed, run onto reels and shipped around the country to be shown for a few wherever desired.

The "service" where such a movie would be shown might seem much like any other service till the time for the message from the Word of God. Then the lights would be put out and the picture turned on. The "message" would consist of this movie. What followed the picture would, of course, vary with the circumstances, but often an invitation song is sung and a tender appeal is made for erring sinners to return to God.

Now, what is wrong with all this? Why should any man object to this or go out of his way to oppose its use in the house of God? Here is my answer.

1. It violates the scriptural law of hearing.

The power of speech is a noble gift of God. In his ability to open his mouth and by means of words make his fellows know what is going on inside his mind, a man shares one of the prerogatives of the Creator. In its ability to understand the spoken word the human mind rises unique above all the lower creation. The gift which enables a man to translate abstract ideas into sounds is a badge of his honor as made in the image of God.

Written or printed words are sound symbols and are translated by the mind into hearing. Hieroglyphics and ideograms were, in effect, not pictures but letters, and the letters were agreed-upon marks which stood for agreed-upon ideas. Thus words, whether spoken or written, are a medium for the communication of ideas. This is basic in human nature and stems from our divine origin.

It is significant that when God gave to mankind His great redemptive revelation He couched it in words. "And God spake all these words" very well sums up the Bible's own account of how it got here. "Thus saith the Lord" is the constant refrain of the prophets. "The words that I speak unto you, they are spirit, and they are life," said our Lord to His hearers (John 6:63). Again He said, "He that heareth my word, and believeth on him that sent me, hath everlasting life" (John 5:24). Paul made *words* and *faith* to be inseparable: "Faith cometh by hearing, and hearing by the word of God" (Romans 10:17). And he also said, "How shall they hear without a preacher?" (Romans 10:14).

Surely it requires no genius to see that the Bible rules out pictures and dramatics as media for bringing *faith* and *life* to the human soul.

The plain fact is that no vital spiritual truth can be expressed by a picture. Actually all any picture can do is to recall to mind some truth already learned through the familiar medium of the spoken or written word. Religious instruction and words are bound together by a living cord and cannot be separated without fatal loss. The Spirit Himself, teaching soundlessly within the heart, makes use of ideas previously received into the mind by means of words.

If I am reminded that modern religious movies are "sound" pictures, making use of the human voice to augment the dramatic action, the answer is easy. Just as far as the movie depends upon spoken words it makes pictures unnecessary; the picture is the very thing that differentiates between the movie and the sermon. The movie addresses its message primarily to the eye, and to the ear only incidentally. Were the message addressed to the ear as in the Scriptures, the *picture* would have no meaning and could be omitted without loss to the intended effect. Words can say all that God intends them to say, and this they can do without the aid of pictures.

According to one popular theory the mind receives through the eye five times as much information as through the ear. As far as the external shell of physical facts is concerned this may hold good, but when we come to spiritual truth we are in another world entirely. In that world the outer eye is not too important. God addresses His message to the hearing ear. "We look," says Paul, "not at the things which are seen, but at the things which are not seen: for the things which are seen are temporal; but the things which are not seen are eternal" (2 Corinthians 4:18). This agrees with the whole burden of the Bible, which teaches us that we should withdraw our eyes from beholding visible things, and fasten the eyes of our hearts upon God while we reverently listen to His uttered words.

"The word is nigh thee, even in thy mouth, and in they heart: that is, the word of faith, which we preach" (Romans 10:8). Here, and not somewhere else, is the New Testament pattern, and no human being, no, and no angel from heaven has any right to alter that pattern.

2. The religious movie embodies the mischievous notion that religion is, or can be made, a form of entertainment.

This notion has come upon us lately like a tidal wave and is either openly taught or tacitly assumed by increasing numbers of people. Since it is inextricably bound up with the subject under discussion I had better say more about it.

The idea that religion should be entertaining has made some radical changes in the evangelical picture within this generation. It has given us not only the "gospel" movie, but a new type of religious journalism as well. It has created a new kind of magazine for church people, which can be read from cover to cover without effort, without thought—and without profit. It has also brought a veritable flood of religious fiction with plastic heroines and bloodless heroes like no one who has ever lived upon this well-known terrestrial ball.

That religion and amusement are forever opposed to each other by their very essential natures is apparently not known to this new school of religious entertainers. Their effort to slip up on the reader and administer a quick shot of saving truth while his mind is on something else is not only futile; it is, in fact, not too far short of being plain dishonest. The hope that they can convert a man while he is occupied with the doings of some imaginary hero reminds one of the story of the

Catholic missionary who used to sneak up on sick people and children and splash a little holy water on them to guarantee their passage to the city of gold.

I believe that most responsible religious teachers will agree that any effort to teach spiritual truth through entertainment is at best futile and at worst positively injurious to the soul. But entertainment pays off, and the economic consideration is always a powerful one in deciding what shall and what shall not be offered to the public—even in the churches.

Deep spiritual experiences come only from much study, earnest prayer and long meditation. It is true that men by thinking cannot find God; it is also true that men cannot know God very well without a lot of reverent thinking. Religious movies, by appealing directly to the shallowest stratum of our minds, cannot but create bad mental habits which unfit the soul for the reception of genuine spiritual impressions.

Religious movies are mistakenly thought by some people to be blessed of the Lord because many come away from them with moist eyes. If this is a proof of God's blessing, then we might as well go the whole way and assert that every show that brings tears is of God. Those who attend the theater know how often the audiences are moved to tears by the joys and sorrows of the highly paid entertainers who kiss and emote and murder and die for the purpose of exciting the spectators to a high pitch of emotional excitement. Men and women who are dedicated to sin and appointed to death may nevertheless weep in sympathy for the painted actors and be not one bit the better for it. The emotions have had a beautiful time, but the will is left untouched. The religious movie is sure to draw together a goodly number of persons who cannot distinguish the twinges of vicarious sympathy from the true operations of the Holy Ghost.

3. The religious movie is a menace to true religion because it embodies acting, a violation of sincerity.

Without doubt the most precious thing anybody possesses is his individuated being; that by which he is himself and not someone else; that which cannot be finally voided by the man himself nor shared with another. Each one of us, however humble our place in the social scheme, is unique in creation. Each is a new whole man possessing his own separate "I-ness" which makes him forever something apart, an individual human being. It is this quality of uniqueness which permits a man to enjoy every reward of virtue and makes him responsible for every sin. It is his *selfness*, which will persist forever and which distinguishes him from every creature which has been or ever will be created.

Because man is such a being as this, all moral teachers, and especially Christ and His apostles, make *sincerity* to be basic in the good life. The word, as the New Testament uses it, refers to the practice of holding fine pottery up to the sun to test for purity. In the white light of the sun all foreign substances were instantly exposed. So the test of sincerity is basic in human character. The sincere man is one in whom is found nothing foreign; he is all of one piece; he has preserved his individuality unviolated.

Sincerity for each man means *staying in character with himself*. Christ's controversy with the Pharisees centered around their incurable habit or moral play acting. The Pharisee constantly pretended to be what he was not. He attempted to vacate his own "I-ness" and appear in that of another and better man. He assumed a false character and played it for effect. Christ said he was a hypocrite.

It is more than an etymological accident that the word "hypocrite" comes from the stage. It means *actor*. With that instinct for fitness which usually marks word origins, it has been used to signify one who has violated his sincerity and is playing a false part. An actor is one who assumes a character other than his own and plays it for effect. The more fully he can become possessed by another personality, the better he is as an actor.

Bacon has said something to the effect that there are some professions of such nature that the more skillfully a man can work at them the worse man he is. That perfectly describes the profession of acting. Stepping out of our own character for any reason is always dangerous and may be fatal to the soul. However innocent his intentions, a man who assumes a false character has betrayed his own soul and has deeply injured something sacred within him.

No one who has been in the presence of the Most Holy One, who has felt how high is the solemn privilege of bearing His image, will ever again consent to play a part or to trifle with that most sacred thing, his own deep sincere heart. He will thereafter be constrained to be no one but himself, to preserve reverently the sincerity of his own soul.

In order to produce a religious movie someone must, for the time, disguise his individuality and simulate that of another. His actions must be judged fraudulent, and those who watch them with approval share in the fraud. To *pretend* to pray, to *simulate* godly sorrow, to *play at worship* before the camera for effect—how utterly shocking to the reverent heart! How can Christians who approve this gross pretense ever understand the value of sincerity as taught by our Lord? What will be the end of a generation of Christians fed on such a diet of deception disguised as the faith of our fathers?

The plea that all this must be good because it is done for the glory of God is a gossamer-thin bit of rationalizing which should not fool anyone above the mental age of six. Such an argument parallels the evil rule of expediency which holds that the *end is everything* and sanctifies the means, however evil, if only the end will be commendable. The wise student of history will recognize this immoral doctrine. The Spirit-led Church will have no part of it.

It is not uncommon to find around the theater human flotsam and jetsam washed up by the years—men and women who have played false parts so long that the power to be sincere has forever gone from them. They are doomed to everlasting duplicity. Every act of their lives is faked, every smile is false, every tone of their voice artificial. The curse does not come causeless. It is not by chance that the actor's profession has been notoriously dissolute. Hollywood and Broadway are two sources of corruption which may yet turn America into a Sodom and lay her glory in the dust.

The profession of acting did not originate with the Hebrews. It is not a part of the divine pattern. The Bible mentions it, but never approves it. Drama, as it has come down to us, had its rise in Greece. It was originally a part of the worship of the god Dionysus and was carried on with drunken revelry.

The Miracle Plays of medieval times have been brought forward to justify the modern religious movie. That is an unfortunate weapon to choose for the defense of the movie, for it will surely harm the man who uses it more than any argument I could think of just offhand.

The Miracle Plays had their big run in the Middle Ages. They were dramatic performances with religious themes staged for the entertainment of the populace. At their best they were misguided efforts to teach spiritual truths by dramatic representation; at their worst they were shockingly irreverent and thoroughly reprehensible. In some of them the Eternal God was portrayed as an old man dressed in white with a gilt wig! To furnish low comedy, the devil himself was introduced on the stage and allowed to cavort for the amusement of the spectators. Bible themes were used, as in the modern movie, but this did not save the whole thing from becoming so corrupt that the Roman Church had finally to prohibit its priests from having any further part in it.

Those who would appeal for precedent to the Miracle Plays have certainly overlooked some important facts. For instance, *the vogue of the Miracle Play coincided exactly with the most dismally corrupt period the Church has ever known.* When the Church emerged at last from its long moral night these plays lost popularity and finally passed away. And be it remembered, *the instrument God used to bring the Church out of the darkness was not drama; it was the biblical one of Spirit-baptized preaching.* Serious-minded men thundered the truth and the people turned to God.

Indeed, history will show that *no spiritual advance, no revival, no upsurge of spiritual life has ever been associated with acting in any form.* The Holy Spirit never honors pretense.

Can it be that the historic pattern is being repeated? That the appearance of the religious movie is symptomatic of the low state of spiritual health we are in today? I fear so. Only the absence of the Holy Spirit from the pulpit and lack of true discernment on the part of professing Christians can account for the spread of religious drama so-called evangelical churches. A Spirit-filled church could not tolerate it.

4. They who present the gospel movie owe it to the public to give biblical authority for their act: and this they have not done.

The Church, as long as she is following her Lord, goes along in Bible ways and can give a scriptural reason for her conduct. Her members meet at stated times to pray together: this has biblical authority back of it. They gather to hear the Word of God expounded: this goes back in almost unbroken continuity to Moses. They sing psalms and hymns and spiritual songs: so they are commanded by the apostle. They visit the sick and relieve the sufferings of the poor: for this they have both precept and example in Holy Writ. They lay up their gifts and bring them at stated times to the church or chapel to be used in the Lord's work: this also follows the scriptural pattern. They teach and train and instruct; they appoint teachers and pastors and missionaries and send them out to do the work for which the Spirit has gifted them: all this has plain scriptural authority behind it. They baptize, then break bread and witness to the lost; they cling together through thick and thin; they bear each other's burdens and share each other's sorrows: this is as it should be, and for all this there is full authority.

Now, *for the religious movie where is the authority?* For such a serious departure from the ancient pattern, where is the authority? For introducing into the Church the pagan art of acting, where is the authority? Let the movie advocates quote just *one* verse, from any book of the Bible, in any translation, to justify its use. This they cannot do. The best they can do is to appeal to the world's psychology or repeat brightly that "modern times call for modern methods." But the Scriptures—quote from them one verse to authorize movie acting as an instrument of the Holy Ghost. This they cannot do.

Every sincere Christian must find scriptural authority for the religious movie or reject it, and every producer of such movies, if he would square himself before the faces of honest and reverent men, must either show scriptural credentials or go out of business.

But, says someone, there is nothing unscriptural about the religious movie; it is merely a new medium for the utterance of the old message, as printing is a newer and better method of writing and the radio an amplification of familiar human speech.

To this I reply: The movie is not the modernization or improvement of any scriptural method; rather it is a medium in itself wholly foreign to the Bible and altogether unauthorized therein. It is play acting—just that, and nothing more. It is the introduction into the work of God of that which is not neutral, but entirely bad. The printing press is neutral; so is the radio; so is the camera. They may be used for good or bad purposes at the will of the user. But play acting is bad in its essence in that it involves the simulation of emotions not actually felt. It embodies a gross moral contradiction in that it calls a lie to the service of truth.

Arguments for the religious movie are sometimes clever and always shallow, but there is never any real attempt to cite scriptural authority. Anything that can be said for the movie can be said also for aesthetic dancing, which is a highly touted medium for teaching religious truth by appeal to the eye. Its advocates grow eloquent in its praise—but where is it indicated in the blueprint?

5. God has ordained four methods only by which Truth shall prevail—and the religious movie is not one of them.

Without attempting to arrange these methods in order of importance, they are (1) prayer, (2) song, (3) proclamation of the message by means of words and (4) good works. These are the four main methods which God has blessed. All other biblical methods are subdivisions of these and stay within their framework.

Notice these in order. (1) Spirit-burdened prayer. This has been through the centuries a powerful agent for the spread of saving truth among men. A praying Church carried the message of the cross to the whole known world within two centuries after the coming of the Holy Spirit at Pentecost. Read the book of Acts and see what prayer has done and can do when it is made in true faith.

(2) Spirit-inspired song has been another mighty instrument in the spread of the Word among mankind. When the Church sings in the Spirit she draws men unto Christ. Where her song has been ecstatic expression of resurrection joy, it

has acted wonderfully to prepare hearts for the saving message. This has no reference to professional religious singers, expensive choirs nor the popular "gospel" chorus. These for the time we leave out of consideration. But I think no one will deny that the sound of a Christian hymn sung by sincere and humble persons can have a tremendous and permanent effect for good. The Welsh revival is a fair modern example of this.

(3) In the Old Testament, as well as in the New, when God would impart His mind to men He embodied it in a message and sent men out to proclaim it. This was done by means of speaking and writing on the part of the messenger. It was received by hearing and reading on the part of those to whom it was sent. We are all familiar with the verse, "*Speak* ye comfortably to Jerusalem, and *cry* unto her" (Isaiah 40:2). John the Baptist was called "The *voice* of one crying in the wilderness" (Matthew 3:3). Again we have, "And I heard a voice from heaven saying unto me, *Write*" (Revelation 14:13). And the apostle John opens his great work called the Revelation by pronouncing a blessing upon him that *readeth* and them that *hear* and keep the *words* of the prophecy and the things which are *written* therein. The two words "proclaim" and "publish" sum up God's will as it touches His Word. In the Bible, men for the most part *wrote* what had been *spoken*; in our time men are commissioned to *speak* what has been *written*. In both cases the agent is a word, never a picture, a dance or a pageant.

(4) By His healing deeds our Lord opened the way for His saving words. He went about doing good, and His Church is commanded to do the same. Faber understood this when he wrote,

> And preach thee too, as love knows how
> By kindly deeds and virtuous life.

Church history is replete with instances of missionaries and teachers who prepared the way for their message with deeds of mercy shown to men and women who were at first hostile but who melted under the warm rays of practical kindnesses shown to them in time of need. If anyone should object to calling good works a method, I would not argue the point. Perhaps it would be more accurate to say that they are an overflow into everyday life of the reality of what is being proclaimed.

These are God's appointed methods, set forth in the Bible and confirmed in centuries of practical application. The intrusion of other methods is unscriptural, unwarranted and in violation of spiritual laws as old as the world.

The whole preach-the-gospel-with-movies idea is founded upon the same basic assumptions as modernism—namely, the Word of God is not final, and that we of this day have a perfect right to add to it or alter it wherever we think we can improve it.

A brazen example of this attitude came to my attention recently. Preliminary printed matter has been sent out announcing that a new organization is in the process of being formed. It is to be called "International Radio and Screen Artists Guild," and one of its two major objectives is to promote the movie as a medium for the spread of the gospel. Its sponsors, apparently, are not modernists but confessed fundamentalists. Some of its declared purposes are: to produce movies "with or without a Christian slant"; to raise and maintain higher standards in the movie fields (this would be done, it says here, by having "much prayer" with leaders of the movie industry); to "challenge people, especially young people, to those fields as they are challenged to go to foreign fields."

This last point should not be allowed to pass without some of us doing a little challenging on our own account. Does this new organization actually propose in seriousness to add another gift to the gifts of the Spirit listed in the New Testament? To the number of the Spirit's gifts, such as pastor, teacher, evangelist, is there now to be added another, *the gift of the movie actor?* To the appeal for consecrated Christian young people to serve as missionaries on the foreign field is there to be added an appeal for young people to serve as movie actors? That is exactly what this new organization does propose in cold type over the signature of its temporary chairman. Instead of the Holy Spirit saying, "Separate me Barnabas and Saul for the work whereunto I have called them" (Acts 13:2), these people will make use of what they call a "Christian talent listing," to consist of the names of "Christian" actors who have received the Spirit's gift to be used in making religious movies.

Thus the order set up in the New Testament is openly violated, and by professed lovers of the gospel who say unto Jesus, "Lord, Lord," but openly set aside His Lordship whenever they desire. No amount of smooth talk can explain away this serious act of insubordination.

Saul lost a kingdom when he "forced" himself and took profane liberties with the priesthood. Let these movie preachers look to their crown. They may find themselves on the road to En-dor some dark night soon.

6. *The religious movie is out of harmony with the whole spirit of the Scriptures and contrary to the mood of true godliness.*

To harmonize the spirit of the religious movie with the spirit of the sacred Scriptures is impossible. Any comparison is grotesque and, if it were not so serious, would be downright funny. To imagine Elijah appearing before Ahab with a roll of film! Imagine Peter standing up at Pentecost and saying, "Let's have the lights out, please." When Jeremiah hesitated to prophesy on the plea that he was not a fluent speaker, God touched his mouth and said, "I have put my words in thy mouth" (1:9). Perhaps Jeremiah could have gotten on well enough without the divine touch if he had had a good 16mm projector and a reel of home-talent film.

Let a man dare to compare his religious movie show with the spirit of the book of Acts. Let him try to find a place for it in the twelfth chapter of First Corinthians. Let him set it beside Savonarola's passionate preaching or Luther's thundering or Wesley's heavenly sermons or Edwards' awful appeals. If he cannot see the difference *in kind,* then he is too blind to be trusted with leadership in the Church of the Living God. The only thing that he can do appropriate to the circumstances is to drop to his knees and cry with poor Bartimaeus, "Lord, that I might receive my sight" (Mark 10:51; Luke 18:41).

But some say, "We do not propose to displace the regular method of preaching the gospel. We only want to supplement it." To this I answer: If the movie is needed to supplement anointed preaching it can only be because God's appointed method is inadequate and the movie can do something which God's appointed method cannot do. What is that thing? We freely grant that the movie can produce effects which preaching cannot produce (and which it should never try to produce), but dare we strive for such effects in the light of God's revealed will and in the face of the judgment and a long eternity?

7. I am against the religious movie because of the harmful effect upon everyone associated with it.

First, the evil effect upon the "actors" who place the part of the various characters in the show; this is not the less because it is unsuspected. Who can, while in a state of fellowship with God, dare to *play* at being a prophet? Who has the gall to *pretend* to be an apostle, even in a show? Where is his reverence? Where is his fear? Where is his humility? Anyone who can bring himself to *act a part* for any purpose, must first have grieved the Spirit and silenced His voice within the heart. Then the whole business will appear good to him. "He feedeth on ashes; a deceived heart has turned him aside" (Isaiah 44:20). But he cannot escape the secret working of the ancient laws of the soul. Something high and fine and grand will die within him; and worst of all he will never suspect it. That is the curse that follows self-injury always. The Pharisees were examples of this. They were walking dead men, and they never dreamed how dead they were.

Secondly, it identifies religion with the theatrical world. I have seen recently in a fundamental magazine an advertisement of a religious film which would be altogether at home on the theatrical page on any city newspaper. Illustrated with the usual sex-bait picture of a young man and young woman in a tender embrace, and spangled with such words as "feature-length, drama, pathos, romance," it reeked of Hollywood and the cheap movie house. By such business we are selling out our Christian separation, and nothing but grief can come of it late or soon.

Thirdly, the taste for drama which these pictures develop in the minds of the young will not long remain satisfied with the inferior stuff the religious movie can offer. Our young people will demand the real thing; and what can we reply when they ask why they should not patronize the regular movie house?

Fourthly, the rising generation will naturally come to look upon religion as another, and inferior, form of amusement. In fact, the present generation Yahwist has done this to an alarming extent already, and the gospel movie feeds the notion by fusing religion and fun in the name of orthodoxy. It takes no great insight to see that the religious movie must become increasingly more thrilling as the tastes of the spectators become more and more stimulated.

Fifthly, the religious movie is the lazy preacher's friend. If the present vogue continues to spread it will not be long before any man with enough ability to make an audible prayer and mentality enough to focus a projector will be able to pass for a prophet of the Most High God. The man of God can play around all week long and come up to Sunday without a care. He has only to set up the screen and lower the lights, and the rest follows painlessly.

Wherever the movie is used, the prophet is displaced by the projector. The least such displaced prophets can do is admit that they are technicians and not preachers. Let them admit that they are not sent men or ordained of God for a sacred work. Let them refuse ordination and put away their pretense.

Allowing that there may be some who have been truly called and gifted of God but who have allowed themselves to be taken in by this new plaything, the danger to such is still great. As long as they can fall back upon the movie, the *pressure that makes preachers* will be wanting. The *habit* and *rhythm* which belong to great preaching will be missing from their ministry. However great their natural gifts, however real their enduement of power, still they will never rise. They cannot while this broken reed lies close at hand to aid them in the crisis. The movie will doom them to be ordinary.

In Conclusion

One thing may bother some earnest souls: why so many good people approve the religious movie. The list of those who are enthusiastic about it includes many who cannot be written off as borderline Christians. If it is an evil, why have not these denounced it?

The answer is, *lack of spiritual discernment.* Many who are turning to the movie are the same who have, by direct teaching or by neglect, discredited the work of the Holy Spirit. They have apologized for the Spirit and so hedged Him in by their unbelief that it has amounted to an out-and-out repudiation. Now we are paying the price of our folly. The light has gone out and good men are forced to stumble around in the darkness of the human intellect.

The religious movie is at present undergoing a period of gestation and seems about to swarm up over the churches like a cloud of locusts out of the earth. The figure is accurate; they are coming from below, not from above. The whole modern psychology has been prepared for this invasion of insects. The fundamentalists have become weary of manna and are longing for red flesh. What they are getting is a sorry substitute for the lusty and uninhibited pleasures of the world, but I suppose it is better than nothing, and it saves by pretending to be spiritual.

Let us not for the sake of peace keep still while men without spiritual insight dictate the diet upon which God's children shall feed. I heard the president of a Christian college say some time ago that the Church is suffering from an "epidemic of amateurism." That remark is sadly true, and the religious movie represents amateurism gone wild. Unity among professing Christians is to be desired, but not at the expense of righteousness. It is good to go with the flock, but I for one refuse mutely to follow a misled flock over a precipice.

If God has given wisdom to see the error of religious shows we owe it to the Church to oppose them openly. We dare not take refuge in "guilty silence." Error is not silent; it is highly vocal and amazingly aggressive. We dare not be less so. But let us take heart: there are still many thousands of Christian people who grieve to see the world take over. If we draw the line and call attention to it we may be surprised how many people will come over on our side and help us drive from the Church this latest invader, the spirit of Hollywood.

Other Titles by A.W. Tozer: